UNIVERSITY OF NORTH CAROLINA
STUDIES IN THE ROMANCE LANGUAGES AND LITERATURES
Number 107

THE ITALIAN VERB
A MORPHOLOGICAL STUDY

THE ITALIAN VERB

A MORPHOLOGICAL STUDY

BY

FREDE JENSEN

CHAPEL HILL

THE UNIVERSITY OF NORTH CAROLINA PRESS

DEPÓSITO LEGAL: V. 4.615 - 1971

ARTES GRÁFICAS SOLER, S. A. - JÁVEA, 28 - VALENCIA (8) - 1971

TABLE OF CONTENTS

	Pages
GENERAL CHANGES IN THE LATIN VERBAL SYSTEM	17
THE INFINITIVE	18
Inchoatives	18
The four conjugations	19
ACCENTUATION	24
THE THEMATIC VOWEL	26
THE THEMATIC CONSONANT	31
THE PRESENT INDICATIVE	36
The present indicative endings	36
The present indicative of a few separate verbs	41
THE PRESENT SUBJUNCTIVE	49
THE IMPERATIVE	52
THE IMPERFECT INDICATIVE	54
THE IMPERFECT SUBJUNCTIVE	57
THE PERFECT (*Passato Remoto*)	60
The weak perfects	60
The strong perfects	65
THE PAST PARTICIPLE	74
The weak past participles	74
The strong past participles	78
THE GERUND AND THE PRESENT PARTICIPLE	82
THE FUTURE	84
THE CONDITIONAL	88
INDEX	91
BIBLIOGRAPHY	96

PREFACE

The present morphological study is intended as a guide to students of Italian Philology. It is designed to show the transformation from Latin verbs into the Old and Modern Italian verbal system. Due consideration has been given, especially for the medieval period, to dialectal developments which, in view of the linguistic fragmentation of the Italic peninsula, are of the greatest importance to any historical study of the Italian language.

Many important works deal with Italian verb morphology: Meyer-Lübke, D'Ovidio and Rohlfs, to mention just a few of the foremost scholars in the field. They have served as constant guides in our research, and we acknowledge our large debt to Gerhard Rohlfs' masterly work in Italian historical grammar. Pierre Fouché's book on French verb morphology has often served us as a model, and we wish to express our gratitude for the inspiration drawn from this source.

The work is inspired by the methods of traditional, historical philology, and its main *raison d'être* is pedagogical. It presupposes little knowledge of Latin morphology, but the reader should be familiar with the basic rules of Italian phonological development.

We are indebted to the Committee on University Scholarly Publications of the University of Colorado for a substantial grant and to Professor Luigi Romeo for his unsparing encouragement and support.

FREDE JENSEN

April, 1970
Boulder, Colorado

Quez el mon non a valensa
Que sa valors no la vensa.

(Peire Vidal)

TO GILLES LOUIS DELISLE

ABBREVIATIONS

CL: Classical Latin.
cond.: conditional.
fut.: future.
Germ.: Germanic.
ind.: indicative.
inf.: infinitive.
imp.: imperative.
impf.: imperfect.
Mon.: Monaci's Crestomazia Italiana.
pf.: perfect.
pers.: person.
plur.: plural.
pres.: present.
sing.: singular.
subj.: subjunctive.
VL: Vulgar Latin.

ABBREVIATIONS OF NAMES OF DIALECTS

Berg.: Bergamo
Calabr.: Calabrian
Cors.: Corsican
Emil.: Emilian
Gen.: Genovese
Ligur.: Ligurian
Lomb.: Lombard
Lucch.: Lucchese
Neap.: Neapolitan

Pad.: Paduan
Piem.: Piedmontese
Pist.: Pistoiese
Pugl.: Apulian
Sard.: Sardinian
Sicil.: Sicilian
Ticin.: Ticinese
Ven.: Venetian.

SIGNS AND PHONETIC SYMBOLS

- . (*under a vowel*): close quality.
- , (*under a vowel*): open quality.
- ¯ (*over a vowel*): long quantity.
- ˘ (*over a vowel*): short quantity.
- ⌒ (*under a vowel*): semivowel, not syllabic.
- / (*over a vowel*): stress.
- ´ and ˋ : used sporadically to indicate close versus open vowel.
- ´ (*over a consonant*): voiced pronunciation.
- * (*before a word*): conjectural, not attested.
- \> and < (*between words*): derivation, the source standing at the open end.
- +: followed by.
- =: equals.
- ñ: palatalized *n*, as in Italian *vigna*.
- dž: palatal affricate, as in Italian *giorno*.
- ə: weak *e*, as in French *double*.
- ü: French *u* in *mur*.

GENERAL CHANGES IN THE LATIN VERBAL SYSTEM

1. Many Classical Latin verb forms were eliminated in Vulgar Latin or in Romance. The passive voice (*amor*) disappeared and with it the complicated system of deponent verbs (*nascor*); only the past participle (*amatus, natus*) was kept and used in the formation of a new analytic passive. The active voice suffered many losses: the imperfect and perfect subjunctive (*amarem, amaverim*), the pluperfect indicative (*amaveram*), the future (*amabo*), the futurum exactum (*amavero*), the future of the imperative (*amato*), the perfect and future of the infinitive (*amavisse, amaturus esse*), the future of the participle (*amaturus*) and the two supines (*amatum, amatu*). This very general outline does, of course, not take into account the survival of some of these forms in various areas of Romania.

2. Through regular phonetic development, many verbal endings became insufficiently clear. *Amabit* (fut.) and *amavit* (pf.) would have evolved to the same phonetic result, as would *scribes* (fut.) and *scribis* (pres. ind), and also *ama(ve)rim* (pf. subj.) and *amarem* (impf. subj.), etc. The resulting confusion was largely remedied through the creation of new, analytic forms, in keeping with a strong trend in Romance towards a periphrastic tense construction. The replacement, in Vulgar Latin and Romance, of the synthetic future (*amabo*) through the periphrasis * *amare habeo*, the creation of a new tense, the conditional (* *amare habebam*, * *amare habui*), and the formation of new perfect tenses by combining an auxiliary verb (*habere*, * *essere*) with the past participle (*avevo fatto, sono venuti*) are examples of this preference for analytic expression in the vernacular.

THE INFINITIVE

3. The four conjugations of Latin are continued in Italian:

1. cantāre > cantare
2. vĭdēre > vedére
3. crēdĕre > crédere
4. partīre > partire.

Both the second and third conjugations have an *e* ending and differ only in accentuation. Modern Italian thus has an *a*, an *e* and an *i* conjugation, these three vowels being thematic in the 2. pers. plur. of the pres. ind. or in the impf. ind.: *cantáte, vedéte, credéte, partíte*; *cantávo, vedévo, credévo, partívo*.

INCHOATIVES

4. In addition to the above categories, the *-ire* conjugation can be either simple (*servire - servo*) or inchoative (*finire - finisco*). The inchoative endings of Classical Latin, *-isco* and *-esco*, were used to express inceptive action: *floreo - floresco, finio - finisco*. In Vulgar Latin, the inchoative endings penetrate into the present tense of many verbs of the *-ire* conjugation. The immediate result of this penetration, which affects only the forms of the present that are stressed on the stem, is a leveling out of the stress pattern:

finio finis finit finimus finitis finiunt
finisco finiscis finiscit finimus finitis finiscunt

Most of the original, inchoative meaning of the *-isco* suffix is lost, though it may still be present, at least to a certain extent, in

THE INFINITIVE

verbs like: *fiorire, rinverdire, aggrandire*. Other verbs are completely void of any inchoative meaning: *capire, preferire, ubbidire*.

Some *-ire* verbs were not affected by the inchoative flexion: *aprire, coprire, avvertire, divertire, dormire, fuggire, partire, pentire, salire, seguire, sentire, servire, uscire, offrire, soffrire, vestire*, etc. Others admit both a simple and an inchoative form: *mento - mentisco, aborro - aborrisco, applaudo - applaudisco, nutro - nutrisco, appaio - apparisco, tosso - tossisco*.

A few verbs which had a simple flexion in Old Italian, became inchoative later on: Old Italian *pato, pero, trado*; Modern Italian *patisco, perisco, tradisco*.

Partire admits either flexion, but the two forms have become semantically differentiated; *parto* is intransitive (= leave), *partisco* is transitive (= share).

THE FOUR CONJUGATIONS

5. *The -āre conjugation*. Numerically this is the strongest conjugation; it is also the most stable in that it suffers few defections and has few new additions.

A few learned words change from *-ĕre* to *-āre*:

consumĕre > consumare
trĕmĕre > tremare.

The change from *prosternĕre* to *prostrare* takes place within Latin on the basis of the perfect and past participle forms: *prostravi, prostratum* (cf. *cantavi, cantatum*).

For Latin *sternutare*, Tuscan has two collateral forms: *sternutare* and *sternutire*.

Old Italian examples of the change from *-ĕre* to *-are* are:

excerpĕre > scerpare
minuĕre > menovare.

As for *fare < facĕre*, this is an irregular verb which has little in common with the *-are* conjugation. *Facĕre* should give **farre* (cf. **tragĕre > trarre*); *fare* is analogical from *dare* and *stare*.

6. *The -ēre conjugation.* Some *-ĕre* verbs changed to *-ēre* in Vulgar Latin:

> *cadĕre* > *cadēre*. Meyer-Lübke explains this change as due to analogical influence from *-ēre* verbs which also have *a* as a thematic vowel, such as *placēre, iacēre, tacēre*.
>
> *sapĕre* > *sapēre*. This verb is strongly influenced by *habēre*. Northern dialects have *aver, saver*; compare also French *avoir, savoir*. Since both verbs have an *-ui* perfect, we get the following analogical ratio: *habuit* : *habēre* :: *sapuit* : *x* (sapēre). In addition to this, the above explanation of how *cadēre* was derived also fits *sapēre*. *Habēre* also influences the Classical Latin infinitives *velle* > VL *volēre, posse* > VL *potēre*.

Old Italian has *capére* < *capĕre*, *offerére* < *offerrĕre* < *offerre*.

Far more common is the transition from *-ēre* to *-ĕre*; many of these changes go back to Vulgar Latin:

> *respondēre* > *rispóndere*; cf. French *répondre*
> *mordēre* > *mórdere*; cf. French *mordre*
> *ridēre* > *rídere*; cf. French *rire*
> *mĭscēre* > *méscere*
> *tergēre* > *térgere*
> *tondēre* > *tóndere*; cf. French *tondre*
> *torquēre* > *torcere > *tórcere*; cf. French *tordre*
> *mŏvēre* > *muóvere*; but French *mouvoir*
> *ardēre* > *árdere*
> *splendēre* > *spléndere*
> *lūcēre* > *rilúcere*; cf. French *reluire*
> *mulgēre* > *múngere*
> *nocēre* > *nuócere*; cf. French *nuire*
> *complēre* > *cómpiere*, and also *compire*.

Other *-ēre* verbs join the *-ire* group. This change was facilitated by the *i* in the 1. pers. sing. of the pres. ind. and in the pres. subj.: *floreo - audio, floream - audiam*, etc.

> *complēre* > *compire*
> *emplēre* > *empire*
> *florēre* > *fiorire*
> *pentēre* > *pentire*. *Pentére* is found in Dante and Boccacio.
> *ad-parēre* > *apparire*. Also *trasparire*, etc. *Apparére* and *sparére* are common in Old Italian.

THE INFINITIVE 21

Iacopo Mostacci has *odere* (= *udire*) (Mon. 44, I, 13), Pier della Vigna uses *sentere* (= *sentire*) (ib. II, 5).

7. *The -ĕre conjugation.* Many verbs changed in Vulgar Latin from *-ēre* to *-ĕre* as seen above: *árdere, mórdere, múngere, rídere, rilúcere, rispóndere.* Specifically for Italian, we have *cómpiere* and *muóvere.*

From the *-ire* conjugation, this group gets a few additions:

redīre > riédere
prurīre > prúdere
ferīre > Old Italian *fiédere*, but Modern Italian *ferire*.

A change from *-āre* to *-ĕre* occurs in *adrogāre* > *arrógere*. This change may have come about through the past participle *adrogĭtus*; cf. *perdĭtus - perdĕre.*

Verbs changing from *-ĕre* to *-are* were treated above (*consumĕre, tremĕre*). For changes from *-ĕre* to *-ire*, see below the *-ire* group. Old Italian still has *cúsere* (= *cucire*), *fúggere, rápere, trádere.*

CL *esse* > VL *essĕre* > *essere*; cf. French *être*.

8. *The -īre conjugation.* Transitions from the *-ire* group into other conjugations have already been dealt with, and likewise the verbs changing from *-ēre* to *-ire*: *fiorire, compire, pentire, putire* (< *putēre*).

In Northern dialects as well as in Sicilian, *ē* phonetically becomes *i*. Examples: Piem. *nuśi* (< *nŏcēre*), Emil. *taśir* (< *tacēre*), Sicil. *avire, dolire, piacire*. The Sicilian forms may spread to the cultured poetry of Tuscany in the Duecento, but *avire* is also encountered in the non-literary Frammenti of 1211. It is normally assessed as a mere graph in this prose text, but Bertoni ascribes it to Southern influence and points to a certain degree of "ibridismo linguistico" in the Frammenti.

Verbs changing from *-ĕre* to *-ire*:

fugĕre > fuggire. This change goes back to Vulgar Latin; cf. French *fuir*. The analogy could be: *finio : finire :: fugio : x (fugire)*. Guido Fava uses the form *fugere*.
consuĕre > cucire. From *cucio* < * *consio*.
As for *morire*, Latin had not only *mŏri* and VL * *morĕre*, but also *morīrī*, found in Plautus and Ovid. Compare

Old Portuguese *morre* and *morrei* which are derived from the *-ĕre* form.

Many verbs of a learned or literary nature show the same change from *-ĕre* to *-ire*; some of these verbs have *-i̯o* in the 1. pers. sing. of the pres. ind.:

>   rapĕre > rapire
>   capĕre > capire
>   concipĕre > concepire.

But this change also affects many verbs that do not have *-i̯o*:

>   applaudĕre > applaudire
>   annuĕre > annuire
>   convertĕre > convertire
>   fallĕre > fallire
>   digerĕre > digerire
>   CL sĕqui > VL * sequĕre, * sequire > seguire
>   CL offerre, sufferre, profferre > VL * offerrĕre, * sufferrĕre, profferrĕre, > offrire, soffrire, profferire. This

isolated group of Classical Latin infinitives is normalized in Vulgar Latin, and the change to the fourth conjugation is then prompted by an analogy with *aperīre > aprire*.

9. Germanic verbs in *-jan* normally join the *-ire* conjugation:

>   * warjan > guarire
>   * warnjan > guarnire
>   * frumjan > fornire
>   * ex-marrjan > smarrire.

An exception is * *waidanjan > guadagnare*; cf. French *gagner*. Germanic verbs in *-an* join the *-are* group: * *wardan > guardare*.

10. *Syncopated infinitives.* Through syncopation of the weak vowel and subsequent consonantal assimilation, a few third conjugation infinitives have *rr* and are isolated in the paradigms; an example is: *ponĕre > * pon're > porre. Porre* is still used, whereas other similar infinitives are antiquated. *Tollĕre > * tol're > torre*; by analogy with this verb as well as with *porre*, we get *sciorre*

(< *sciogliere*), *corre* (< *cogliere*), *scerre* (< *scegliere*). Also still in use is *trarre* < * *tragere* < *trahere*; the change to * *tragere* is caused by an analogy with *agere*: *actum* : *agere* :: *tractum* : *x* (*tragere*). In the same fashion, we should have expected * *farre* (< *facĕre*) and * *dirre* (< *dīcĕre*); *fare* and *dire* are analogical from the normal infinitive endings, *fare* perhaps more directly so from *dare* and *stare*.

ACCENTUATION

11. A shift in stress from stem to ending occurs in the 1. and 2. pers. plur. of the present indicative of -*ĕre* verbs:

véndĭmus > vendémo > vendiamo
véndĭtis > vendéte.

This change is due to a direct imitation of the other conjugations which all have stressed endings here.

The stress moves towards the beginning of the word in imperfect subjunctives:

canta(vi)ssémus > cantássimo
canta(vi)ssétis > cantáste
scribissémus > scrivéssimo
scribissétis > scrivéste.

In compound verbs, the stress shifts from prefix back to stem in Vulgar Latin, a process known as recomposition:

démorat > VL demórat > dimora
rétĭnet > VL retĕ́net > ritiene
dísplĭcet > VL displácet > dispiacè
récĭpit > VL recépit > riceve.

In many instances, the original vowel was restored in Vulgar Latin (*retĕ́net, displacet,* in accordance with *tĕ́net* and *placet*), but this did not occur where the derivation had become unclear (*recĭ́pit* had ceased to be felt as a compound of *capit*).

The stress is maintained if the notion of composition is lost; the stem vowel may be syncopated when in a weak position (post-tonic non-final):

cólligit > *coglie*
* *de-éx-citat* > *desta*
* *ex-éligit* > *sceglie*
cólligo > *colgo.*

There may be some oscillation as to stress in learned words: *évito - evíto, írrito - irríto*, etc.

THE THEMATIC VOWEL

12. The vowels ĕ and ŏ diphthongize in an open, stressed syllable; this gives rise to the apophony (or vocalic alternation) *ie - e*, *uo - ò*, according to whether the stem is stressed or not. Examples of the *ie - e* apophony:

> sĕ́det > siede; sĕdḗbat > sedeva; sĕdḗre > sedere
> tĕ́net > tiene; tĕnḗbat > teneva; tĕnḗre > tenere
> vĕ́nit > viene; vĕnī́bat > veniva; vĕnī́re > venire
> rĕ́dit > Old Italian riede; rĕdī́bat > rediva
> fĕ́rit > fiere (fiede); fĕrī́bat > feriva (fediva).

Other instances of pretonic *e* are: *sediamo, sedete, seduto*, etc.

13. Old Italian shows the same apophony in verbs like:

> crĕ́pat > criepa; crĕpáre > crepare
> trĕ́mat > triema; trĕmáre > tremare
> * prĕ́cat > priega; * prĕcáre > pregare
> gĕ́mit > gieme; * gĕmĕ́re áio > gemerò.

But in all these cases, *ie* is reduced later on to *e* according to phonetic rules: *ie > e* when following a mute + *r*, or when following a palatal. The original apophony is replaced by an *ę - ę* alternance, where the tonic vowel is open, the pretonic close: *pręga - pręgare*.

14. In other verbs, analogical influences will level out the vocalic alternance; the infinitive seems to play an important role here as an additional determining factor in the selection of one form over the other:

THE THEMATIC VOWEL

quáerit > chiede; quáerĕre > chiedere. By analogy, we get *chiedeva < quaerēbat. Cherendo* is found in Giacomo da Lentino (Mon. 41, V, 195).

mĕtĕre > mietere; mĕtit > miete. Mieteva < mĕtēbat is analogical.

nĕgáre > negare; nĕgábat > negava. Nega, from Old Italian *niega < nĕgat,* is obtained by analogy.

**sĕquíre > seguire;* **sĕquíbat > seguiva. Segue* from Old Italian *siegue <* *sĕquit is analogical.

sĕcáre < segare; sĕcábat > segava. By analogy, we get *sega < sĕcat,* but in this case, the existence of an alternate form, *sĭcat,* has been attested in inscriptions.

lĕváre > levare; lĕvat > lieva, and then *leva* by analogy. An alternance of *ę - ẹ* is retained.

vĕtat > vieta; vĕtáre > vietare. Here, the stem-stressed vowel has won out, completely replacing pretonic *e.*

15. Since pretonic *e* (< *ē, ĭ, ĕ*) becomes *i* in Italian (ex.: *mĕliŏre > migliore; sēcūru > sicuro*), we should expect to find numerous examples of a vocalic alternation between *i* and *ie, e*; however, the only attested examples of this apophony are limited to the verb *gettare*. Pulci still observes the distinction between *getta* and *gittare, gittò,* and Modern Italian has both *gettare* and *gittare*. The fact that this particular apophony is limited to this one verb makes it desirable to attempt another explanation of the alternance; it would seem that the change to *i* could more legitimately be ascribed to direct influence from the preceding *i̯* (cf. *iunĭperu > ginepro*). In Old French, *iectare has not given a uniform result either; besides *jeter,* we find *jitier* and other variants. In Italian, *e* is generalized from the stem-stressed forms: *cercare, pesare* from *cerca, pesa.*

16. Examples of the *uo - o* apophony:

dŏlet > duole; dŏlēbat > doleva; dŏlēre > dolere
sŏlet > suole; sŏlēbat > soleva; sŏlēre > solere
vŏlet > vuole; vŏlēbat > voleva; vŏlēre > volere
**mŏrit > muore (more);* **mŏrībat > moriva;* **mŏrīre > morire.*

In many verbs, the diphthong has penetrated into the pretonic syllable, thus giving rise to collateral forms both of which may be in common usage, although the analogical form is sometimes condemned by grammarians.

CL nŏcĕre > VL nŏcĕre > nuocere; nŏcet > nuoce; nŏcĕbat > noceva, nuoceva
CL cŏquĕre > VL cŏcĕre > cuocere, cocere; cŏcit > cuoce, coce; cŏcĕbat > coceva, cuoceva. In this particular verb, o has also penetrated into the stem-stressed forms.
CL mŏvĕre > VL *mŏvĕre > muovere, movere; mŏvet > muove; mŏvĕbat > moveva, muoveva
sŏnat > suona; sŏnáre > sonare; sŏnábat > sonava, suonava
*ex-cŏtĕre > scuotere; *ex-cŏtit > scuote; *ex-cŏtĕbat > scoteva, scuoteva.

17. The original apophony is lost in prŏbat, *trŏpat after the reduction of uo to o following a mute + r:

prŏbat > pruova > prova; prŏbáre > provare
*trŏpat > truova > trova; *trŏpáre > trovare.

It is replaced by an alternance of ǫ and ọ: prǫva, prọvare. Uo is generalized in nuotare and vuotare: nuota, nuotava, nuotiamo, vuota, vuotava, vuotiamo, etc., perhaps in order to separate these two verbs from their homonyms notare and votare. O, on the other hand, is generalized in volare: vola, voliamo, etc., and in coprire: copre, coprire. Old Italian has cuopre < *cŏperit.

18. Pretonic o does not normally give u in Italian verbs; even the oldest texts mostly contain only o forms: coprire, soffrire. The same is true, in most cases, of pretonic au: lodare < laudare, osare < ausare, where o is generalized from the stem-stressed forms in preliterary times. But one case of the au - u ablaut has survived into Modern Italian as o - u, with o as the stressed and u as the pretonic vowel; odo (< *audo < audio) - udiamo (< audīmus). We thus have odi, ode, odono as opposed to udite, udire, udito. To this may be added the generalization of u in rubare (< *raubare < Germ. *raubôn), which gives us the analogical form ruba (< *raubat) instead of *roba. Rohlfs and D'Ovidio both list chiudere as another example in question, but the etymology of this verb is not claudere, but rather cludere from the Latin prefixed forms with weakened

thematic vowel: *includere, excludere*. Compare *iactare* as opposed to *proiectare, iniectare*.

The change of *o* to *u* in pretonic position is, of course, a normal trend in Italian (cf. *cucire*) and is quite common in the dialects (Rohlfs lists *durmire, suffrire, murire* for the dialect of Arezzo). Standard Tuscan has leveled out the vocalic alternation by generalizing one of the two vowels, usually *o* from the stressed forms.

19. A couple of verbs show a *ju - i* ablaut: *a(d)iutare* and * *dis(ie)iunare*.

> *a(d)iútat* > *aiuta*
> *a(d)iutábat* > *aitava*.

Analogy has worked in both directions to level out this difference through the creation of new forms: *aita, aiutava. Aitare* is found in the Breve di Montieri (Mon. 30, 39) and in Cielo d'Alcamo (Mon. 61, 110) who also has *aitano* (ib. 111); the analogical form, *aiutare*, is encountered in Paganino da Serezano (Mon. 47, 3). Rainerio da Perugia has: *si v'aiuti Deu* (Mon. 35, 35), but also: *si Deu t'aiti* (ib. 150). Eventually, the *iu* forms won out in Italian, probably through the added influence of the noun *aiuto*, but a few traces are still left of the *i* forms: *aita, aitante*. Compare the Old French flexion of this verb: *aju - aidier*.

> * *dis(ie)iúnat* > *digiuna*.
> * *dis(ie)iunábat* > *desinava*.

On the basis of these two developments, two separate verbs are created. From *digiuna* is derived a new infinitive, *digiunare*; from *desinare* new stem-stressed forms are developed: *desino, desina*, etc. This same split into two separate verbs also occurs in French: *déjeuner* and *dîner*.

20. *Mangiare*. Meyer-Lübke assesses *mandúca* (< *mandúcat*) - *manicare* (< *manducáre*) as a direct analogy from *digiuna - desinare*. These verbs are, of course, closely associated in meaning. The *d* may or may not be retained: *manduca - manuca, mandicare - manicare*. The Ritmo Cassinese has *mandicate* (v. 76), *manduca* (v. 78), *mandicare* (v. 90); the Ritmo di San Alessio has *manicava* (v.

245), and *manicare* is found in Folcacchiero (Mon. 55, 23). A weak vowel *e* is seen in the participle *mandegao*, used by Barsegapé.

Modern Italian *mangiare* shows influence from French *manger*. In fact, all the verbs containing the *iu - i* ablaut have as their counterpart in the French flexional system, a conjugation based on vowel addition: *manju - mangeons, aju - aidons*, etc. It is possible that these verbs have undergone some Northern influence. In the case of *aiutare* > *aitare*, Italian syncopates the vowel as does French; in *manduco - manicare*, Italian weakens the vowels ($u > i$), whereas French drops it altogether. It should be pointed out that the elimination of weak, intertonic vowels is not a characteristic feature of standard Tuscan.

21. Isolated cases of apophony are *deve - dovere*, where labialization occurs in the pretonic position only, and *esco - usciamo, uscire*, where only the pretonic *e* is affected by the analogy with * *ustiu* (< *ōstiu*). As a result, we get a weak versus a strong vowel just like in the previous groups.

THE THEMATIC CONSONANT

22. We are here mainly concerned with problems pertaining to palatalization, based on the different treatment *c* and *g* undergo according to the nature of the following vowel. The presence or absence of a yod will also account for major phonetic differences within a given paradigm. In many cases, these differences are carried into Modern Italian, while other verbs tend to level them out through analogical influence.

23. *The thematic consonant is palatalized by a yod.* The hiatus vowel of the endings *-eo, -io* will cause a palatalization of the thematic consonant and thus create verb forms that differ widely from the parts of the paradigm that sustain no such influence. Compare *vĭdeo > veggio* and *vĭdet > vede*.

By analogy with verb forms without $\underset{\cdot}{i}$, many verbs will simply drop the palatal:

>   *tĭmeo > * temo > temo*
>   *servio > * servo > servo*
>   *dormio > * dormo > dormo.*

24. $C + \underset{\cdot}{i} > cc\underset{\cdot}{i}$; $g + \underset{\cdot}{i} > gg\underset{\cdot}{i}$; $r + \underset{\cdot}{i} > \underset{\cdot}{i}$; $p + \underset{\cdot}{i} > pp\underset{\cdot}{i}$. Examples:

>   *taceo > taccio*
>   *placeo > piaccio*
>   *noceo > noccio*
>   *faciam > faccia*
>   *fugio > fuggio.* A collateral form, *fuggo*, seems to have developed early. Guittone has *fugo* (Mon. 76, V, 3).
>   *pareo > paio*
>   ** mŏrio > muoio*
>   *sapiat > sappia*

sapio > *sappio. This is the form we should expect, but it is not encountered, *Saccio* is from the dialects of the South where *pi̯* normally gives *cci̯*. Used outside of the Southern regions, there is, of course, a possibility of *saccio* being analogical from *faccio*. For other forms (*so, saio*), see the present tense of *sapere*.

25. B + i̯ > bbi̯:

habeat > *abbia*

debeo > Old Italian *debbio*. *Devo* is analogical from *devi* (< *dēbes*), *deve* (< *dēbet*); in turn, *devo* will influence *debbio* making it lose its *i̯*. More generally speaking, one might say that the reduction of *debbio* to *debbo* reflects a strong trend in Italian. *Debbo* is found in Giacomo da Lentino (Mon. 41, III, 55) and in the Registro Lucchese of 1268 (Mon. 128, 19) which also has *debo* (ib. 137). Old Tuscan *deggio* comes from VL* *deio*, analogical from * *aio* < *habeo*. Southern Italian dialects have *deggio, deggiu* through regular phonetic development, since, in the South, *bi̯* > *ggi̯*. *Deg(g)io* is found in Giacomo da Lentino, Ruggerone di Palermo, Rinaldo d'Aquino.

habeo. For a full treatment of this verb form, see the present tense of *habere*.

26. D + i̯ > ggi̯:

vĭdeo > *veggio*. *Vedo* is analogical from *vedi* (< *vĭdes*), *vede* (< *vĭdet*).

sĕdeo > *seggio*. *Siedo* is analogical from *siedi* (< *sĕdes*), *siede* (< *sĕdet*).

* *cadeo* > *caggio*. *Cado* is derived from *cadi, cade* (< *cades, cadet*).

Through the creation of analogical forms (*veggio* > *vedo*; *caggio* > *cado*), the palatal can spread to verbs that have *d* in the 1. pers. sing. of the present indicative instead of *di̯*:

crēdo > Old Tuscan *creggio*

claudo > * *clūdo* (with *u* from *clūdere*; cf. *excludere*) > *chiudo* and Old Tuscan *chiuggio*

quaero > *chiedo* and Old Italian *chieggio*. The *d* of *chiedo* is obtained from *chiedere* < *quaerĕre* by dissimilation, or else it is due to formal influence of *perdere, vendere*, etc.

fiedo (the *d* is from *fiedere* < * *fĕrĕre* < *ferīre*) has an Old Italian variant *feggio*. *Feggiono* is encountered in the Romanzo di Tristano (Mon. 130, 282).

More difficult to explain is the subsequent loss of the palatalization that affects many of the above-mentioned forms in *-ggio* (ex.: *veggio* > *veggo*). Old Italian has *veggo, caggo, seggo, chieggo, fieggo, creggo*; the Sienese dialect has *chiuggo* and *deggo* (< *deggio* < * *deio* < *debeo*). This development may have been touched off by the early change of *fuggio* to *fuggo*. The more general loss of *i̯* in verbs like *dormio, servio, sentio* is, no doubt, to be considered too early a phenomenon to have exerted any direct influence here. The most plausible explanation would appear to be a formal imitation of the many verbs that have a *-go* ending by regular phonetic development or by way of analogy: *frango, giungo, vengo, tengo*.

27. N + i̯ > *gn* (a palatalized *n*):

vĕnio > *vegno* > *vengo*
tĕneo > *tegno* > *tengo*
remaneo > *rimagno* > *rimango*.

The origin of the change of *vegno* to *vengo*, etc., is to be sought in an analogy with a series of verbs that have *-ngo*: *frango, giungo, piango*. The lack of a uniform result of *ng* before a palatal vowel is, no doubt, a decisive factor in this analogy. We get an alternance between *ndž* and *ñ* as evidenced in the Old Italian infinitive variants *piagnere* and *piangere, fignere* and *fingere*. Many modern dialects still have *ñ*. Collateral forms like *spengo - spegno* have further facilitated the transition of *vegno* into this group. The change to *ng* will also affect the 3. pers. plur. where *vengono, tengono, rimangono* are analogical from *frangono, piangono*, etc.

Vengno is found in Giacomino Pugliese (Mon. 57, II, 66), and *bengo* is already found in the Ritmo Cassinese (v. 40). The palatalized root may spread to other verb forms; Guido Fava uses the past participle *vegnuto* (Mon. 34, IV, 17) alongside with *venuta* (ib. IX, 10). A palatalized variant of *tenere* is fairly common in Old Italian: *tegnir* (Mon. 69, 52), *mantignere* (ib. 34, IV, 18), and there are several examples of *tengno, tiegno* in the old language. *Rimangno* is encountered in Rinaldo d'Aquino, *remagno* in Guido Guinizelli.

Pongo (CL *pōno*) is analogical from this whole group of verbs. *Teneva* : *tengo* :: *poneva* : *x* (*pongo*).

28. $L + i\!\!\!/ > gli\!\!\!/$ (a palatalized *l*):

salio > *saglio* > *salgo*
valeo > *vaglio* > *valgo*
dŏleo > *doglio* > *dolgo*
sŏleo > *soglio*
vŏleo > *voglio*.

A *-go* ending is obtained in some verbs of this group by analogy with *colgo* < *collĭgo* and in line with the general trend outlined in the previous paragraph. *Soglio* and *voglio* remain unchanged, and the older form *vaglia* is retained in *vaglia postale*. The old palatalized root of *salio, doleo, valeo* is frequently encountered in the early texts: Iacopo Mostacci has *dolglio* (Mon. 43, 35), Guittone has *dolglia* (Mon. 76, I, 6), and other examples are *vagla* (Mon. 173, 175), *vaglian* (Mon. 79, II, 23). Tommaso da Faenza uses the infinitive *saglire* (Mon. 109, 38) which has an analogical palatalized *l*; cf. French *saillir*.

29. A spread of the *-go* ending is also evidenced in *tolgo* and *sciolgo* which are probably influenced by the verb *colgo* with which they share a morphological agreement in the past participle and the perfect: *colto, tolto, sciolto*; *colsi, tolsi, sciolsi*. This same impact is felt in the infinitive where CL *tollere*, which is kept in the Sienese dialect, becomes *togliere* in Italian, modeled after *cogliere*. The same analogy gives us *sciogliere* from ** ex-solvere*. Other instances of an analogical *-go* ending are: *volvo* > *volgo*, and ** ex-vello* > *svello, svelgo*.

30. The thematic consonant is c *or* g. C and g are retained in front of *a, o* and *u*, but are palatalized before *e* and *i*. This phonetic difference is evident in the *e* and *i* conjugation: *dico, dici, dice*; *mungo, mungi, munge*. The *a* conjugation, on the other hand, generalizes the velar sound: *pago, paghi, paga*; *manco, manchi, manca*. In this conjugation, the velar sound is much stronger numerically than in the other two. Besides, Rohlfs believes the retention of *c* and *g* in the 2. pers. sing. of the present indicative to be linked with the old ending -*as*; *c* and *g* remained even after an analogical -*i* was substituted for the original ending.

The difference between *cuoco* and *cuoci, cuoce* is leveled out by the creation of an analogical *cuocio* (and also *cuociono*) which completely replaces *cuoco* < *cŏco. Boccaccio still uses *coco*. *Nuoccio* < *nŏceo* had beside it in Old Italian a form *nuoco* which may be drawn from *cuoco*. *Exeo* does not give *escio, but *esco*, analogical from *cresco, conosco, nasco*. An analogical *eschi* is found in Dante (Inf. 32, 113); *conoscio* is fairly common in the dialect of Elba. For Old Umbrian, *dichi, dichiamo, dichiate* are attested.

Outside of the realm of palatals and velars, little need be said concerning the thematic consonant. In *quaerĕre* > *chiedere*, *fĕrĕre > *fiedere*, the *d* is due to a dissimilation of *r* - *r* or to a formal influence of *perdere, vendere*, etc. This *d* is then carried into the present stem of these verbs: *chiedo, fiedo*.

THE PRESENT INDICATIVE

THE PRESENT INDICATIVE ENDINGS

31. *The 1. pers. sing.*

1. *canto* > *canto*
2. *vŏleo* > *voglio*
3. *scrībo* > *scrivo*
4. *servio* > * *servo* > *servo.*

The Latin ending *-o* is retained. Southern dialects close it to *-u* or show a weakened *ə*; *-o* is lost in Northern dialects in agreement with Gallo-Romance evolution.

Sŭm > Old Italian *son* > *sono*, by analogy with the regular ending. This is the only Latin verb that does not end in *-o* in the 1. pers. sing.

32. *The 2 pers. sing.*

1. *cantas* > *canti*
2. *vĭdes* > *vedi*
3. *scrībĭs* > *scrivi*
4. *servīs* > *servi.*

The Latin endings are *-as*, *-ēs*, *-ĭs*, *-īs*; they all give *-i* in Italian, but only after a period of hesitation between *-i* and *-e*. Since Italian drops final *s*, *-īs* of the fourth Latin conjugation becomes *-i* by normal phonetic development, and the other conjugations then adopt *-i* by analogy. Meyer-Lübke and D'Ovidio see in *-i* the normal phonological outcome, not only of *-is*, but also of *-as*, *-ēs*, whereas

-*ĭs* gives *-e*, thus accounting for the hesitation, in the old language, between *-i* and *-e*. This theory has now mostly been abandoned.

Some areas of Northwestern Tuscany (Lunigiana, Garfagnana) have the ending *-a* from *-as*: *tu canta, manda*, etc. One factor that may have contributed largely to the decline of the *-a* ending is that it fails to distinguish between the 2. and the 3. pers. sing.

The *-e* ending appears in Old Tuscan texts; in the Divina Commedia, however, *-e* (< *-as*) is used only in rhyme: *tu gride, pense, favelle, preghe, note*. That this *-e* should come from final *a* through regular phonetic development is very unlikely. It is probably analogical from the *e* conjugation, but the final analogy with the *i* conjugation takes place relatively early, since there are examples of *i* already in the oldest texts. Old Sienese has carried *-e* into the *i* conjugation: *tu serve, dorme*, etc.

33. *The 3. pers. sing.*

   1. *cantat* > *canta*
   2. *vĭdet* > *vede*
   3. *crēdĭt* > *crede*
   4. *sentĭt* > *sente*.

The 3. pers. sing. endings are regular: *-a* in the *-are* group, *-e* elsewhere. The dental consonant is lost.

34. *The 1. pers. plur.*

   1. *cantāmus* > Old Italian *cantamo* > *cantiamo*
   2. *vĭdēmus* > Old Italian *vedemo* > *vediamo*
   3. *crĕdĭmus* > VL *credémus* > Old Italian *credemo* > *crediamo*
   4. *sentīmus* > Old Italian *sentimo* > *sentiamo*.

Classical Latin has: *cantámus, vĭdĕmus, crĕdĭmus, sentīmus*. An early Vulgar Latin change of *crĕdĭmus* to *credémus* levels out the difference in accentuation that separates the *-ĕre* conjugation from the other groups. Through regular phonetic development, the three Vulgar Latin endings, *-ámus, -émus, -ímus*, are then continued into Old Italian as *-amo, -emo, -imo*. These three endings are still found in the dialects of Umbria, Lazio and Le Marche, according to Rohlfs who, for Assisi, gives the forms: *lavamo, vedemo, partimo*.

Old Tuscan texts already have the modern ending *-iamo*, mainly in lieu of *-imo* which is rarely found in Tuscan. It also supplants *-amo* rather early, whereas *-emo* is still very much alive in the Tuscan texts of the Trecento. Dante has: *sapemo, vivemo, tenemo, potemo, volemo, vedemo*, etc., and all three endings, *-amo, -emo* and *-imo*, are common in Old Pisan and Lucchese texts.

Modern Italian has generalized the subjunctive ending *-iamo* throughout, a development which, for central Tuscany, is completed about the middle of the 14th century. The morphological point of contact between the indicative and the subjunctive, capable of bringing about the penetration of *-iamo* into the indicative, could be *semo* < *sĭmus* which replaces *sŭmus* at a very early date. When *semo* becomes *siamo* (< * *sĭamus*), this new form retains its dual function as subjunctive and indicative. It is generally assumed that *siamo* will then influence *stare, dare* and *andare*, giving rise to the new forms: *stiamo, diamo, andiamo*. But this explanation has certain weaknesses, since *semo* and *diamo* are used concurrently in the same text, which seems to prove that we already had a *diamo*, before *semo* became *siamo*.

An additional element that would help account for the penetration of a subjunctive ending into the indicative is the rather close relationship that exists between an interrogative indicative and an exhortative subjunctive. This usage may first affect a common exhortation like *eamus* > *giamo*; *sagliamo* and *stiamo*, which are closely related in meaning, are soon created, and the analogy could spread from there.

Cases of *-iano* are found in older Tuscan texts: Brunetto Latini, Pulci, Ariosto, etc.; Dante, on the other hand, criticizes *facciano*. The origin of this *n* is to be sought in the apocopated verb form, followed by *ci* or *ne*, where a partial assimilation would explain the change to a dental: *vedianci, andianne, andiancene*.

35. *The 2. pers. plur.*

1. *cantatis* > *cantate*
2. *vĭdētis* > *vedete*
3. *crēdĭtis* > VL *credētis* > *credete*
4. *sentītis* > *sentite*.

THE PRESENT INDICATIVE 39

In Vulgar Latin, the stress shifts from stem to ending in the -*ĕre* group under analogical pressure from the other conjugations; this is parallel to the change from *crédĭmus* to *credémus*. The three sets of endings thus obtained, -*átis*, -*étis*, -*ítis*, are all regularly continued in Italian.

Boiardo uses an -*i* as the last part of the ending, which is, no doubt, dialectal: *ascoltati, stati*, etc. There are numerous dialectal developments. In Sicilian, -*étis* and -*ítis* merge into -*iti*: *aviti, putiti, vuliti, partiti, veniti*. Northern dialects have -*ai*, -*e* < -*atis* and -*i* < -*etis*, -*itis*: Piem. *porté*, Ven. *lavé*, Old Lomb. *pensé, trové, volí, saví, deví, odí, serví*.

36. The 3. pers. plur.

1. *cantant* > *cantano*
2. *vĭdent* > VL *vidunt* > *vedono*
3. *crēdunt* > *credono*
4. *sentiunt* > VL *sentunt* > *sentono*.

Vulgar Latin seems to have given preference to the -*unt* ending over -*ent*; examples of *vidunt, debunt, abunt* (= *habent*) abound in legal documents from Tuscany of the 8th century. The loss of *i̯* in the fourth conjugation (* *sentunt*, * *dormunt*, * *servunt*, * *partunt*) is pan-Romance. We are thus left with the two endings -*ant* and -*unt* which should have given * -*an* and * -*on* (* *cantan*, * *senton*), yet even the oldest texts show the addition of an epenthetic vowel -*o* (*cantano, sentono*). Various factors have combined in this evolution which essentially reflects a strong trend in Italian to avoid consonantal endings (cf. *cuore, miele* < CL *cŏr, mĕl*). The -*o* is usually considered a vocalic resonance of the preceding vowel (*crēdunt* > *credon* > *credono*). It is clear, however, that a simple vocalic resonance would give us *cantant* > * *cantan* > * *cantana* (compare Sard. *kantana*) and not *cantano*, but Italian standardized the use of -*o* as an epenthetic or paragogical vowel; cf. Lausberg's statement: "Jedoch traten bald Uniformierungen ein" (in: *Romanische Sprachwissenschaft* § 528). This standardization in Italian dates back to preliterary times, since * *cantana* remains a purely hypothetical form. A variety of reasons favor the choice of -*o*. We have already seen -*unt* replace -*iunt* and -*ent*, thus becoming the normal ending of three conjugations. This numerical strength is further reinforced by the very common verb *sono* < *sŭnt*, which gets its *-o* by analogy with *sono* < *sŭm*, where *-o* is a morphological addition and not a case of epenthesis. Both *sŭm* and *sŭnt* had regularly become *son* in Old Italian, and this accounts for the fact that an *-o* added to one form will also affect the other.

The accentuation pattern is of the greatest importance in any discussion of epenthesis, since not only vowel addition, but also the treatment of the final consonant *n* (< *-nt*) are directly related to the position of the stress. The oxytonic stress, which occurs only in monosyllables, is instrumental in the doubling of *n* as well as in the epenthesis of *-o*: *dant* > *danno*. This, incidentally, constitutes yet another proof that *sono* from *sŭnt* is largely of analogical origin; if not, we should expect *sonno* which is a rare form in Old Italian. The paroxytonic stress also causes epenthesis, but the *n* is not doubled: *crēdunt* > * *credon* > *credono*. Proparoxytones, on the other hand, do not show vowel addition, and the *n* is dropped because of the weak position: *fécĕrunt* > *fecero*, and not * *fecerono*. One might add here that verb forms like *fecero, amassero* may also have contributed to the choice of an *-o* epenthesis.

The explanation of *-o* as being epenthetic is already found in Diez. A different explanation is offered by Förster who derives the *-o* from archaic Latin forms: *danunt* (= *dant*), *solinunt* (= *solent*), etc. On the basis of such forms, Förster derives a popular * *vendunt* > *vendono*, with the loss of *n* because of proparoxytonic stress. In the same fashion, he establishes forms like * *amanunt*, * *sunt*, etc. D'Ovidio warns against attaching too much importance to obscure archaic Latin forms, and he rightly points out that *danunt* should give * *dano* and not *danno* (cf. *manu* > *mano*; *sĭnu* > *seno*, etc.).

The epenthetic vowel may be dropped in a syntactic group: *dicon di sì*.

37. *Dialectal variants of the 3. pers. plur. endings.* In Old Tuscan texts, *-ono* is sometimes used in the *a* conjugation instead of *-ano*. Old Sienese has *cantono, portono*, and Machiavelli uses *tirono. Ballono, saltono, cantono* are forms used by Lorenzo dei Medici.

THE PRESENT INDICATIVE 41

Vulgar Tuscan *vendano, dormano* reflect a common phonetic treatment of the weak post-tonic vowel, esp. before a nasal; cf. *pampĭnu* > *pampano*, and also *chronica* > *cronaca*.

The Lucchese dialect has *-eno* in the *e* and *i* conjugations: *temeno, senteno*. Lombard and Venetian drop the final vowel: *cantan, venden*, and even *n* may be dropped: *canta, vende*. This leads to complete identity between singular and plural, and in these same areas, *è* may even replace *sono*.

Southern dialects mainly have a *-u* ending: Calabr., Sicil. *cantanu, cantunu*. There is also, as shown by these two examples, some oscillation in the weak post-tonic vowel.

THE PRESENT INDICATIVE OF A FEW SEPARATE VERBS

38. *The present tense of essere.*

> *sŭm* > *son* > *sono*. The addition of *-o* is analogical from *canto, sento*, etc. *Son* is common in Old Italian; it is found in Giacomo da Lentino (Mon. 41, III, 49) and in Mon. 45, I, 3. A variant, *sun*, is attested in Mon. 116, III, 23. A proclitic form, *so*, is quite common, too, in the old language; it is encountered in the Confessione Umbra (Mon. 6, 1), in Giacomo da Lentino (Mon. 41, VII, 50) and in Stefano Protonotaro (Mon. 89, I, 12) who also has *su* (ib. II, 18). Guittone uses *sone* at the end of a line (Mon. 76, I, 50); Barsegapé has *sonto* (Mon. 70, 155).
>
> *ĕs* > *ei*, and Modern Italian *sei*. The etymological form is encountered in Guido Fava (Mon. 33, XIII, 1 and 34, VI, 2) and in Iacopone (Mon. 160, II, 14). Guido Fava also uses the apocopated form *e'* (Mon. 34, VI, 3). The present tense of the verb *essere* presents a set of forms with *s-* and another set with the strong root *es-*; it is analogical influence from the *s* group which gives us a form *sĕs > *siei, sei*. *Siei* is found in vulgar Tuscan, but is relatively rare; *sei* originates from proclitic usage of the verb (cf. *ĕram* > *iera, era*). One of the earliest examples of *sei (sey)* is found in the Laude (Mon. 159, III, 42), and the apocopated form *se'* appears in Mon. 59, I, 34 as well as in Cielo d'Alcamo (Mon. 61, 127).
>
> *ĕst* > *è*. Old Italian also has *este, esti*, Southern forms according to Rohlfs. Very common in the old language

is another epenthetic form: *ene*. It appears in the Confessione Umbra, the Breve di Montieri, the Laudes Creaturarum, etc.

sŭmus > *somo*. This etymological form is rare; it appears in Guido Fava (Mon. 34, IX, 4) and Giacomo da Lentino (Mon. 41, V, 162). *Sŭmus* was replaced very early by the subjunctive form *sĭmus* > *semo*; this form is very common in Dante as well as in earlier texts and is still used by Ariosto. Venetian has *semo*, Lombard *sèm* or *sém*. *Siamo* goes back to a new Vulgar Latin subjunctive form **siamus*; this change is analogical from the subjunctives of the second and fourth conjugations which both end in *i̯* + *-amus* in the 1. pers. plur. (cf. *moneamus, audiamus*). Rohlfs points to the more precise analogy of *habeamus*. A need for having a clear division between root and ending may have touched off the change to begin with (cf. *sto* > ** sta-o*; *do* > ** da-o*). A form *siemo*, found in the Tristano (Mon. 130, 125), is explained by Wiese as a contamination of *semo* and *siete*. Rohlfs believes that *semo* was pronounced with *ę*, and that *siemo* therefore is but a diphthongized variant. This latter explanation is, of course, also based on an analogical influence of forms with *ę* (*sei, siete*) to begin with. A rather general spread of the thematic vowel *ę* (*ęs, ęst, ęstis*) would thus help explain the frequency of open *ę*.

ĕstis > ** sĕtis* > *siete*. Rohlfs mentions a Northern Calabrian form, *èsə*, as a remnant of *ĕstis*. Elsewhere, *ĕstis* is replaced by an analogical *s*- form, ** sĕtis* (cf. *ĕs* > ** sĕs*) > *siete*. The proclitic form *sete* is found in the Ritmo Cassinese (v. 96) and also in Ariosto where D'Ovidio explains it as due to analogical influence from *semo*.

sŭnt > *son* > *sono*. The *-o* is analogical from *sono* < *son* <*sŭm* rather than epenthetic in origin, as already outlined in § 36. Oxytonic stress should lead to a doubling of *n*, yet the form *sonno* is rare; it occurs in Mon. 65, 154 and Mon. 149, 20. *Sonto* is a Franco-Venetian form (Mon. 167, 320). Common in Dante and also found in Guido Fava is *enno*, formed from *è* on the basis of *ha - hanno, fa - fanno, fe - fenno*. Uguccione da Lodi has the apocopated form *èn* (Mon. 62, 8).

39. *The present tense of avere.*

habeo > *VL * aio* > Old Tuscan *aggio*. This form, which is very common in the old language, represents a regular

THE PRESENT INDICATIVE 43

development in Tuscan of intervocalic *i*. Its Southern
counterpart is *aggiu*. *Aio* is a common form in the old
poetic language; it appears in the Ritmo di San Alessio
(v. 2) and in the Ritmo Cassinese (v. 15). Old Sienese
and Old Lucchese have *abbo, abo*; these forms occur in
the Ricordi di Matasala Senese and in the Registro
Lucchese del 1268. They are common in Cecco Angiolieri
and Albertano da Brescia and found also in Dante (Inf.
32,5: *io non l'abbo*). *Abbo* could be analogical from
debbo or from a ratio like: *cantiamo* : *canto* : : *abbiamo* : *x* (*abbo*), but it is mostly explained as a
reduction of * *abbio* (< *habeo*) to *abbo* (cf. *fuggio* >
fuggo; *debbio* > *debbo*). It presupposes a continuation
of CL *habeo*, possibly in the upper classes of society.
* *Abbio* is a hypothetic form.

Aço is encountered in Stefano Protonotaro (Mon. 89, I, 41); it
is probably a Venetian form and could be analogical from *saçço*, a
form used by Iacopo Mostacci.

The modern form *ho* is based on an analogy with *do* and *sto*.
Dai, da : *do* : : *hai, ha* : *x* (*ho*). It is already common in Dante.

habes > VL * *as* > *hai*
habet > VL * *at* > *ha*. The form *ave*, regularly developed
from CL *habet*, is not uncommon in the old language;
Rohlfs terms it a "Lentoform" as compared with *ha*. It
occurs in the Ritmo di San Alessio (v. 71), in the Frammenti of 1211, in Cielo d'Alcamo (Mon. 61, 145), and is
found later on in Dante, Petrarca and Tasso.
habēmus > *avemo*. This is the standard Old Italian form,
of which *avimo*, *avimu* are Southern variants. The modern form, *abbiamo*, is originally a subjunctive (< *habeamus*); it appears already in the Frammenti of 1211
(Mon. 27, 15) alongside with *avemo* (ib. 273).
habētis > *avete*. The Southern variants are *avite, aviti*;
Vulgar Tuscan has *ete* with omission of the initial *av-*.
habent > VL *habunt* > * *haunt* > *on, onno*. These forms
are used in Arezzo and Umbria; compare also French
ont < * *haunt*. Modern Italian *hanno* is analogical from
danno; a dialectal variant is *ano*.

40. *The present tense of stare.*

sto > VL * *stao* > *sto*. *Sto* does not go directly back to
CL *sto*, but is based on an extended VL form * *stao* with

restoration of the stem vowel *a*, followed by the usual
-o ending. In Italian, * *stao* regularly gives *sto*, since *ao*
comes to be the equivalent of the diphthong *au*; cf. Old
Provençal *estau* and *dau*. Old Sicilian has *stao*, Modern
Sicilian *staju*, analogical from *aju* < * *aio*. Rohlfs mentions a variety of dialectal forms, based on various
analogies: Southern Lazio has *stongo*, analogical from
dongo < * *donio* with a *-go* ending; the Abruzzese form
stengo is drawn from *vengo*; Old Ven. *stago* could be
influenced by *fago*.

stas > *stai*

stat > *sta*. Neap. *stace*, Calabr. *staci* are drawn from *face*.

stamus > *stamo* > *stiamo*

statis > *state*

stant > *stanno*. *Stano* is used in Western Tuscan dialects.
Umbrian has *stonno*, analogical from *honno*.

41. *The present tense of* dare. The evolution of *dare* parallels that of *stare*, to which the reader is referred for specific explanations.

do > VL * *dao* > *do*. The South has *dao* and *daju*; other
dialectal forms are: *dongo, dengo, dago*, besides *don*
< *dōno*.

das > *dai*

dat > *da*. Barese and Old Neap. *dacə* is by analogy with
face.

damus > *damo* > *diamo*

datis > *date*

dant > *danno*. Western Tuscan dialects have *dano*, Umbrian has *donno*.

42. *The present tense of* vadere, andare, ire. The present tense of *vadere* is defective, comprising only stem-stressed forms. The 1. and 2. pers. plur. are normally derived from *andare*, although some dialects use *ire*. The thorny problem concerning the etymology of *andare* cannot be dealt with here.

vado > *vado*. Old Tuscan and Neap. have *vao*; cf. *sto*
and *do*. The form *vo* is analogical from *do* and *sto*, and
these verbs will influence the other *vadere* forms, too.
Old Ligur. and Old Ven. have *vago* from *fago*; Sicil.
has *vaju*.

vadis > *vai*. *Vai* is analogical from *dai, stai, hai*.

vadit > *va*. By analogy with *da, sta, ha*.

andamus > *andamo* > *andiamo*. Umbrian has *gimo*, Sicil. *imu*.

andatis > *andate*. Umbrian has *gite*, Sicil. *iti*.

vadunt > VL * *vaunt* (analogical from * *haunt*) > *vonno*. This form is used by Dante and found in the dialects of Arezzo and Umbria; cf. *honno*. Modern Italian *vanno* is analogical from *danno* and *stanno*. *Vano* exists in Elba and Versilia.

The Umbrian forms *gimo, gite* derive their initial palatal from the subjunctive *giamo* < *eamus* from where it could easily spread to other forms; cf. the infinitive *gire*.

43. *The present tense of fare.*

facio > *faccio*. Calabr. has *fazzu*; *faço* appears in Guido Fava and Mostacci. *Fo* is analogical from *do, sto, ho*. Ligur. *fagu* is based on * *faco* < *facio*.

facis > *faci*. This form is common in Dante; the modern form *fai*, based on *dai, stai, hai*, is already encountered in Giacomino Pugliese.

facit > *face*. Used by Dante, *face* disappears before an analogical *fa*, from *da, sta, ha*. Guido Fava uses an epenthetic form: *fae*.

facimus > *facciamo*. Phonetically, we should expect *facemo* (after a VL shift in accent), but examples of this form are rare: Mon. 137, 20 has *faceme*, the Calabr. dialect has *facimu*. The modern form is found in the Novellino. *Famo* is analogical from *damo, stamo*; *faemo* appears in the Lettera Senese of 1260 (Mon. 74, 56).

facitis > Calabr. *faciti* and Modern Italian *fate*. *Fate* cannot represent the regular phonetic development; Calabr. *faciti* is more faithful to the original Latin etymon. *Fate* is probably drawn from *state, date*; cf. the infinitive *fare* which is based on *stare, dare*.

faciunt > Old Italian *facciono*. Modern Italian *fanno* is from *danno, stanno*. *Fonno*, which exists in Arezzo and Umbria, is based on *onno*.

44. *The present tense of potere.* CL *posse* is replaced by *potere* : *habuit* : *habere* : : *potuit* : *x* (*potere*). But Italian continues *possum* and *possunt* and also has forms with *ss* in the subjunctive (cf. French *puis, puisse*).

possum > *posso*. The South has continuations of *pŏteo* > Neap. *pozzə*, Calabr. *puozzu*; Cielo d'Alcamo uses *pozzo* (Mon. 61, 131). Also found in the old language is *poi* (Galliziani da Pisa in Mon. 53, 19). It is, no doubt, based on *voi*, collateral form of *voglio* < *vŏleo*.

pŏtes > Old Italian *puoti* > *puoi*. The shortening is due to proclitic usage; in addition, the verb has undergone analogical influence of *vuoi*.

pŏtet > Old Italian *puote* > *può* (proclitic shortening). Cellini has *puole* which reflects influence of *vuole*.

pŏtēmus > *potemo* > *possiamo*. The *-iamo* ending is substituted for Old Italian *-emo*, and the root is analogical from the 1. pers. sing. *posso*. Old Italian also has *potiamo* with the *pot-* root retained; Mon. 174, 157 has an example. *Possemo* is used by Barsegapé (Mon. 70, 118) and is also found in Old Bergman. (Mon. 141, 83).

pŏtētis > *potete*

possunt > *possono*. *Ponno* is analogical from *onno*; the diphthong of *puonno* comes from *può*. Ristoro d'Arezzo uses both *puono* (Mon. 139, 171) and *ponno* (ib. 124). Occasional forms, going back to the *pot-* root, are also encountered in the old language: *poten* in Brunetto Latini (Mon. 97, II, 15), *potinu* in Mon. 173, 79, *pozzon* in Cielo d'Alcamo (Mon. 61, 21). Straparola has *puolono*; cf. the 3. pers. sing. *puole*.

45. *The present tense of volere. Volere* replaces CL *velle* : *habuit* : *habere* : : *voluit* : *x* (*volere*).

vŏleo > *voglio*. *Voi* is not uncommon in the 1. pers. sing. in the old language; it is used by Giacomo da Lentino, Paganino da Serezano, Girardo Pateg, Re Enzo, etc.

vŏles > Old Italian *vuoli* > *vuoi* (proclitic usage). Meyer-Lübke explains *vuoi* as originating from *vuogli* with the palatalized *l* of *voglio*; *vuogli* is then reduced to *vuoi* if used before a consonant (*vuogli amare* - *vuoi cantare*).

vŏlet > *vuole* (*vole*)

vŏlēmus > *volemo* > *vogliamo*

vŏlētis > *volete*

vŏleunt > *vogliono*. *Voleno* is found in Mon. 151, 1; it seems to be a continuation of *volent*, otherwise not continued for Italian. Dialectal *vonno* is based on *onno*; Sicil. has *vonnu*.

THE PRESENT INDICATIVE

46. *The present tense of sapere.* This verb is strongly influenced by *dare, stare* and *avere.*

sapio should give * *sappio.* The etymological form has not been attested; instead, Old Italian has *saccio* which is essentially a Southern form (cf. Sicil., Calabr. *sacciu*), or else it could possibly be drawn from *faccio. Saccio* is found in Giacomo da Lentino, Cielo d'Alcamo, Guglielmo Beroardi; Rinaldo d'Aquino uses *sacio.* Old Italian also shows numerous examples of *sazzo* (Cielo d'Alcamo), *saço* and *saçço* (Iacopo Mostacci). By analogy with VL * *aio* < *habeo,* we obtain a form * *saio* which has also been continued in Italian: *sayo* (Mon. 157, 147), Piem. *sai.*

The modern form *so* is analogical from *do, sto* and *ho. Sao* could represent an intermediate stage of this development; this is the famous form we find in the Placito Capuano and the Placito di Teano. Grayson mentions other examples of *sao* in Iacopo Mostacci, Tomaso da Faenza and Chiaro Davanzati.

sapes > Old Italian *sapi. Sai* is drawn from *dai, stai* and *hai.*
sapet > Old Italian *sape.* This form is encountered in Rinaldo d'Aquino and Giacomo da Lentino and is used by Dante. Iacopo Mostacci has both *sape* and *sa* (Mon. 43, 22; ib. 29). Calabr. *sape,* Sicil. *sapi.* The modern form *sa* is based on *da, sta* and *ha.*
sapēmus > *sapemo* > *sappiamo.* Meyer-Lübke also quotes *savemo,* analogical from *avemo*; a Sicil. form *savimu* is found in Mon. 173, 89.
sapētis > *sapete. Savete,* analogical from *avete,* appears in Giacomo da Lentino (Mon. 41, II, 10).
sapent > * *sapeno.* The etymological form is hypothetic, but a Sicil. text (Mon. 172, 28) offers *sapinu,* and the Northern Calabr. dialect has *sapənə. Sanno* is from *hanno, danno* and *stanno.*

47. *The present tense of dovere.*

debeo > *debbio.* There does not appear to be any examples of the etymological form in Monaci. The most common form in Old Tuscan is *deggio* < * *deio,* VL form of *debeo*; cf. *habeo* > VL * *aio.* In Sicil., *deggiu* is the phonetic continuation of *debeo; deio* < VL * *deio* is used in the Canzoni di Re Federico. *Debbo* comes from *debbio* through a process that has already been discussed in detail. *Devo* is analogical from *devi* (< *dēbes*) and *deve* (< *dēbet*).

dēbes > *devi*. *Dei* is a proclitic form used sporadically in the old language.

dēbet > *deve*. Proclitically, we get *dee*, contracted into *dé*; it is used by Guido Fava. Through a different development, a stressed *e* in hiatus may change to *i*; the resulting form, *die*, is quite common in the Frammenti of 1211.

debēmus > *dovemo* > *dobbiamo*. *Devem*, with the non-labialized root, is encountered in the old Sermone Gallo-Italico.

debētis > *dovete*

VL *debunt* > *deono*. The *b* would tend to disappear before *u*, giving us the form *deono* which is attested in Old Sienese (Mon. 64, 14: *ellino deono venire*). Old Tuscan tends to raise *e* in hiatus to *i* as seen above (*die*); the Frammenti has *dion dare*. *Debono* is derived from *debbo*, *devono* from *devo*.

THE PRESENT SUBJUNCTIVE

48. *The -are conjugation.*

cantem > cante > canti
cantes > cante > canti
cantet > cante > canti
cantēmus > cantemo > cantiamo
cantētis > cantete > cantiate
cantent > canteno (?) > cantino.

The three sing. forms in *-e* are all attested for Old Tuscan. Dante uses them; in the 2. pers., however, *-e* appears only in rhyme, a fact which points to archaic usage. A couple of examples: *fa che di noi alla gente favelle* (Inf. 16, 85); *onde un poco mi piace che m'ascolte* (ib. 20, 57). Petrarca uses *-e* in the 1. and 3. pers. sing., *-i* in the 2. pers. sing. Meyer-Lübke and D'Ovidio consider *-i* the phonetic norm (< *-ēs*); Rohlfs, on the other hand, suggests the traditional analogy with *-īs* just like in the indicative: "Es dürfte wohl die gleiche Quelle haben wie das *-i* der zweiten Person des Indikativs" (G. Rohlfs: *Historische Grammatik der Italienischen Sprache* § 555). Chronologically, it seems quite clear that *-i* first penetrates into the 2. pers. sing. from where it then spreads to the entire singular by analogy.

In the 1. pers. plur., *-emo* is replaced by *-iamo*. The extension of *-iamo*, in preliterary times, to the present subjunctive of all verbs is, in Grandgent's words, "puzzling". Rohlfs believes *-iamo* (and *-iate*) to represent the phonetic norm in the other conjugations from where it then penetrates into the *-are* group (*op. cit.* § 555). However, this is much too general a statement. It is obvious, first of all, that an exception must be made in regard to the *-ĕre* conjugation, since it has no i: *scribamus* gives *scrivamo*, not *scriviamo*. And moreover, the i that appears in the *-ēre* and *-īre* conjugations (*timeam, sentiam*, etc.) is very often eliminated at a very early stage in the evolution of Italian or Romance. Can we at all assume that i was dropped in other verb forms, but retained in *-iamus* and *-iate* alone? The fact that the thematic consonant remains unaffected by the following i seems to point to an analogical origin of the *-iamo* ending (we have *udiamo* and not **uggiamo, sentiamo* and not **senzamo, partiamo* and not *parzamo, etc.). It would therefore seem advisable to point to more precise analogies here, as does Lausberg (*op. cit.* § 803) who derives *-iamo* from *habeamus, sapiamus* and *siamus. The main impact would probably come from *siamus, and the magnitude of its role would be comparable to that of *sŭmus* > *sons* in forming the French verbal ending *-ons*.

Vulgar Tuscan often uses the indicative endings *-amo, -emo, -imo* and *-ate, -ete, -ite* in the subjunctive.

In the 2. pers. plur., *-ete* is replaced by *-iate*, a development which is parallel to the change from *-emo* to *-iamo*. The influence felt is that of CL *sĭtis* > VL *siatis > *siate*.

In the 3. pers. plur., *cantent* should give *canteno; *cantino* has the *i* of the singular, or else the *i* is due to the weak position.

49. *The -ēre conjugation.*

  tĭmeam > *tema*
  tĭmeas > *tema*
  tĭmeat > *tema*
  tĭmeamus > *temiamo*
  tĭmeatis > *temiate*
  tĭmeant > *temano*.

The i was lost early. Some hesitation affects the 2. pers. sing. in the old language; it often ends in *-i*, and there are also cases of *-e*, whereas Modern Italian has *-a* throughout in the singular.

50. *The -ĕre conjugation.*

  scrībam > *scriva*
  scrības > *scriva*
  scrībat > *scriva*

THE PRESENT SUBJUNCTIVE 51

scrībāmus > *scrivamo* > *scriviamo*
scrībātis > *scrivate* > *scriviate*
scrībant > *scrivano*.

Here also, *-i* and *-e* occur in the 2. pers. sing.: *tu dichi, tu facci, aprende, rende*. *Scrivino*, analogical from *cantino*, is criticized by purists in the 16th century.

51. *The -ire conjugation.*

sentiam > *senta*
sentias > *senta*
sentiat > *senta*
sentiamus > *sentiamo*
sentiatis > *sentiate*
sentiant > *sentano*.

The *i* was lost early. There are likewise here cases of *-i* and *-e* in the 2. pers. sing.

52. *Old Tuscan subjunctive forms.* Dante uses the following subjunctive forms of some common verbs: *debbia, vegna, tegna, rimagna, caggia, veggia, aggia, deggia, vaglia*. Most of these forms are analogical from the 1. pers. sing. of the present indicative: *temo* : *tema* :: *veggio* : *x* (*veggia*). Parallel to this example are *caggia, aggia, deggia*; and the Old Tuscan subjunctives *vegna, tegna, rimagna* are derived from *vegno, tegno, rimagno* in the same fashion. A similar analogical development gives us *possa* from the indicative *posso*. *Aggia* and *deggia* can, of course, go directly back to the shortened VL forms * *aia* and * *deia*.

Stet > * *ste* > *stea* > *stia*, and *det* > * *de* > *dea* > *dia*, are analogical from *sia*, and Cors. *fia* (= *faccia*) is similarly derived. The old language sometimes uses proclitic forms of these verbs: *die, stie, fie*. Old Italian *tria*, subjunctive of *trarre*, is analogical from *dia*.

Aia (= *abbia*) is a Southern form; it is based on *aio*, common in the South as a 1. pers. sing. of the present indicative. Dante uses *aia* in rhyme. Old Sienese *abba* is obtained from *abbo*, and *sappa* (= *sappia*) is then modeled on *abba*.

THE IMPERATIVE

53. *The 2. pers. sing.*

1. *canta > canta*
2. *vĭdē > vede > vedi*
3. *scrībĕ > scrive > scrivi*
4. *salī > sali.*

Canta and *sali* are kept, whereas the *-e* ending of the second and third conjugations is replaced by *-i*, analogical from *sali* or stemming from the general spread of *-i* in the 2. pers. sing. Modern Italian has *vedi, temi, metti,* etc. These *-i* forms are encountered as early as in the Novellino, but old texts from Northern Italy seem to have kept the *-e* somewhat longer; Rohlfs quotes examples from Bonvesin and Barsegapé. Southern Italian dialects replace *-e* by *-i*, as is to be expected.

Fa and *va* are drawn from *sta* (< *sta*) and *da* (< *da*). Vulgar Tuscan uses *stai, dai, fai, vai,* taken from the 2. pers. sing. of the present indicative with which the imperative has strong formal ties.

54. *The 2. pers. plur.*

1. *cantāte > cantate*
2. *vĭdēte > vedete*
3. *scrībĭte > VL scribéte > scrivete*
4. *sentīte > sentite.*

These imperatives all show identity with the corresponding forms of the present indicative; in fact, it is not possible to decide whether they are direct continuations of the old Latin imperative, or whether they are borrowed from the present indicative. Compare French

THE IMPERATIVE   53

which uses the indicative: *chantez* < *cantatis,* and Spanish which keeps the two forms separated: *cantad* < *cantate* and *cantáis* < *cantatis.*

In the third conjugation, we have the usual change in stress from stem to ending. *Fate* is analogical from *date* and *state* or derived from *fa,* just like *dite* is based on *di.* The plural form corresponding to *va* is *andate.*

Northern dialects have: *-ate* > *-ae* > *-ai* > *-e* (*mandé* = *mandate*). In the South, where *e* regularly becomes *i, -ete* and *-ite* merge into *-iti*: Sicil. and Calabr. *viditi, vinniti* (= *vendete*).

55. *The 1. pers. plur.* The 1. pers. plur. of the present subjunctive is used to express an exhortation. In Southern dialects where the present subjunctive is lost, the indicative will normally assume this function (Calabr. *cantamu, facimu*), and Rohlfs points to widespread confusion between indicative and subjunctive in this role. The difference between the two moods is not always morphologically clear because of the *-iamo* ending.

56. *Other subjunctive forms used as imperatives.* The use of the subjunctive in the role of an imperative is not limited to the 1. pers. plur. Some verbs, which are not normally used in commands, derive their whole imperative from the present subjunctive: *siate, abbiate, sappiate, vogliate.* Compare French *soyez, ayez, sachez, veuillez.* In the singular, these verbs normally have an *-i* ending: *sii* (and an older form *sie*), *abbi, sappi, vogli.* These are probably old subjunctive forms; Grandgent considers them subjunctives which have been given the normal imperative ending *-i* (*abbia* > *abbi, sia* > *sii*). There are other examples in Old Italian and in the dialects of subjunctives used in imperative function; cf.: *una caosa me dicate* (Ritmo Cassinese, v. 57).

THE IMPERFECT INDICATIVE

57. The first conjugation has *-abam*, the second and third have *-ebam* in Latin: Cases of *-iebam* in the third conjugation (*faciebam*, etc.) gave way to *-ebam*, and in the fourth conjugation, *-iebam* is replaced by *-ibam* which already existed in early Latin.

The final *-i* of the 2. pers. sing. is analogical from the present indicative; this is a very early change.

1. *-are*:

      cantābam > *cantava* > *cantavo*
      cantābas > *cantavi*
      cantābat > *cantava*
      cantabămus > *cantavamo*
      cantabătis > *cantavate*
      cantābant > *cantavano*.

2. *-ēre*:

      vĭdēbam > *vedeva* > *vedevo*
      vĭdēbas > *vedevi*
      vĭdēbat > *vedeva*
      vĭdebămus > *vedevamo*
      vĭdebătis > *vedevate*
      vĭdēbant > *vedevano*.

3. *-ĕre*:

      scrībēbam > *scriveva* > *scrivevo*
      scrībēbas > *scrivevi*
      scrībēbat > *scriveva*
      scrībebămus > *scrivevamo*[a]

scrībebătis > scrivevate
scrībēbant > scrivevano.

4. -ire:

partiēbam > partibam > partiva > partivo
partiēbas > partibas > partivi
partiēbat > partibat > partiva
partiebămus > partibámus > partivamo
partiebătis > partibátis > partivate
partiēbant > partibant > partivano.

58. In the 1. pers. sing., an analogical -o from the present indicative replaces the original -a (-ava > -avo, etc.). This change occurs relatively late; it is not reflected in Dante, Petrarca or Boccaccio, but, on the other hand, we already find it in Iacopone, and later on in Pulci and Cellini. The original -a ending is still used by Goldoni, Leopardi and Foscolo, whereas Manzoni generalizes the use of -o. Rohlfs suggests that the change to -o may have originated in the provinces of Siena and Lucca.

In the 2. pers. sing., the -i ending was obtained at a very early date. The etymological ending is encountered in Garfagnana and Lunigiana (ex.: *tu tə lavava*). Old Tuscan texts sometimes have -e (*cantave*), in accordance with the old present tense ending (*tu cante*).

By adopting these changes in the 1. and 2. pers. sing., Italian has obtained a system of phonetically distinct forms throughout the imperfect tense.

Some areas of Tuscany move the stress further back in the 1. and 2. pers. plur.: *cantávamo, finívate*, etc. The use of *-ano* instead of *-amo* (Machiavelli has: *noi solaváno*) has an exact parallel in the present; it originates in the apocopated form, followed by *ne* or *ci*.

Some zones of Tuscany show the penetration of *-eva* into the *a* conjugation: Lucch. *devo* (= *davo*), *stevo, andevo*. For the *e* and *i* groups, forms without -v- are common in Old Italian: *-ea* = *-eva*, *-ia* = *-iva*. The origin is to be sought in dissimilated forms of *habebam* and *debebam* in Vulgar Latin: *abea, debea*. Compare the French imperfect endings which are obtained in exactly the same way. Dante uses *-ea* and *-eva*, *-ia* and *-iva*; particularly common is *-ea* which occurs with greater frequency than *-eva*. Examples: *dovea, sedea, avea, partia, venia*, etc. These forms are also frequent in Old Sienese and Old Umbrian. The loss of -v- is rare in the *a* conjugation.

In Sicil. and Calabr. where *ē* becomes *i*, the imperfects of the *e* and *i* conjugations are not kept apart: *vidiva* (= *vedeva*), *viniva* (= *veniva*). In the Old Tuscan poetic language, *-ia* is used in the *e* conjugation due to Sicilian influence: *avia, tenia, credia*.

Especially in Arezzo and Siena, the 3. pers. *-ia* and *-iano* developed into *-ie* and *-ieno* with a subsequent change in stress to the more open vowel: *-iè, -ièno*. Some of these forms are found in Dante who has *faciensi* (Par. 18, 77), *moviensi* (ib. 79), *movièno* (Purg. 10, 81). Grandgent ascribes the change in stress to influence of the common dipthong *ie*.

59. *The imperfect of essere: Latin ĕram.*

>   *ĕram* > *era* > *ero*
>   *ĕras* > *eri*
>   *ĕrat* > *era*
>   *ĕramus* > dialectal *éramo* > Tuscan *eravámo*
>   *ĕratis* > dialectal *érate* > Tuscan *eraváte*
>   *ĕrant* > *erano*.

This verb being mainly proclitic, the non-diphthongized forms win out over *iera*, etc. However, both forms occurs in Old Tuscan: *iera* is found in the Frammenti of 1211, in the Tesoretto and also in Vita Nuova. *Eravámo* and *eraváte* are analogical from the regular imperfect formation (*cantavámo*, etc.) which has a stressed ending in the 1. and 2. pers. plur. Lucca and Pisa have *éramo* and *érate*. A further analogy from *eravámo* gives *avavámo* and a few other formations with the added syllable *-va-*.

THE IMPERFECT SUBJUNCTIVE

60. The Italian imperfect subjunctive is derived from the Latin pluperfect subjunctive (*cantavissem, audivissem*) which, in Vulgar Latin, had replaced the old imperfect subjunctive (*cantarem, audirem*). The syllable -*vi*- is dropped: *cantavissem* > *cantassem*, *audivissem* > *audissem*, and the endings obtained for the *a*, *e* and *i* conjugations are -*assi*, -*essi* and -*issi*, etc.

1. CL *cantavissem* > VL *cantásse(m)* > Old Italian *cantasse* > *cantassi*
2. *debuíssem* > Old Italian *dovesse* > *dovessi*
3. CL *perdidíssem* > VL *perdesse(m)* > Old Italian *perdesse* > *perdessi*
4. CL *partivíssem* > VL *partisse(m)* > Old Italian *partisse* > *partissi*.

Strong perfect verbs (*vīdī, fēcī, rūpī, scrīpsī, dīxī*, etc.) form their imperfect subjunctive with the root of the present tense: *vedessi, facessi, rompessi, scrivessi, dicessi*.

In the 1. pers. sing., *assem, -essem, -issem* are continued in Old Italian as -*asse*, -*esse*, -*isse*. Dante has: *io credesse* (Inf. 13, 25), *io scendesse* (Purg. 8, 46), and in Guittone, we find: *eo trovasse, dovesse, volesse*. The Modern Italian -*i* endings (-*assi*, -*essi*, -*issi*) are analogical either from the perfect indicative (*vidi, feci*) or from the present subjunctive of the *a* conjugation (*canti*). Due to the protracted coexistence of -*e* and -*i* forms in the old language, -*i* also spreads to the 3. pers. sing.

In the 2. pers. sing., -*asses*, -*esses*, -*isses* soon acquire an -*i* ending (-*assi*, -*essi*, -*issi*) in line with other verb forms (present indicative, perfect indicative, imperfect indicative, etc.).

In the 3. pers. sing., the etymological endings *-asse* (< *-asset*), *-esse* (< *-esset*) and *-isse* (< *-isset*) are kept. The old language shows numerous encroachments of the *-i* ending here, since the rest of the singular has *-i*. This development may have been started off by the hesitation between *-e* and *-i* in the 1. pers. sing.; besides, some formal analogy from the present subjunctive where all three forms of the singular are identical, can hardly be excluded.

A change in stress affects the 1. and 2. pers. plur.: *canta(vi)ssémus* > ** cantássemus, canta(vi)ssétis* > ** cantássetis*. This shift is analogical from the singular (*cantássem, cantásses, cantásset*) as well as from the 3. pers. plur. (*cantássent*), and it brings about a uniform accentuation in this tense. The 1. pers. plur. endings are *-ássimo, éssimo, -íssimo* (*cantássimo, vedéssimo, salíssimo*) with weakening of *e* to *i* in post-tonic non-final position. The 2. pers. plur. endings are *-aste, -este, -iste* (*cantaste, vedeste, saliste*) with syncopation of the weak vowel (< *-ássetis, éssetis, -íssetis*). The Lucchese dialect preserves this weak vowel: *cantássite* (= *cantaste*). The old language sometimes makes use of *-assi, -essi, -issi* in order to avoid identity with the passato remoto; an example of this: *acciò che voi non credessi* (Decam. 3, 6).

In the 3. pers. plur., *-ássent, -éssent, -íssent* regularly gave *-ásseno, -ésseno, -ísseno*. These endings are common in Old Italian which also has occurrences of *-ono* instead of *-eno* (cf. present indicative *vedono, partono*). Sacchetti has *fossono, avessono*; Dino Compagni has *potessono*, Cellini *facessino* (with weak vowel *i*). The modern endings *-ássero, -éssero, -íssero* are analogical from the passato remoto (*ebbero, dissero*, etc.). Old Tuscan texts may even show a merger of these two endings: *dovesserono, potesserono*. The most common Tuscan form in the 13th - 14th centuries was *-ono*; *-ero* was borrowed from the strong perfect in the 13th century.

Dante has *venesse* for *venisse*, probably due to *tenesse*. In Southern dialects, we find the usual merger of the *e* and *i* conjugations.

61. *The imperfect subjunctive of essere*: *fŭissem*. Modern Italian has: *fossi, fossi, fosse, fossimo, foste, fossero*. An alternate form, used by Dante and also later writers, is: *fussi, fusse, fussimo, fussero*. This stem vowel is drawn from the perfect *fui*. Both *fosse* and *fusse* are used in the Frammenti of 1211.

62. The old Latin imperfect subjunctive is retained in Sardinian: *levaret, serviret, fakeret*. There are no cases for Italian; Rohlfs (*op. cit.* § 564) refutes Gamillscheg's interpretation of certain verb forms in Cielo d'Alcamo's Contrasto, showing them to be infinitives or conditionals.

THE PERFECT (*PASSATO REMOTO*)

63. There are two main categories of perfect formations, referred to as the weak and the strong perfects. The weak perfects are stressed throughout on the characteristic vowel of the ending (ex.: *cantái, cantásti*); the strong perfect group contains verbs which in some persons accent the root, in others the ending (ex.: *féci - facésti*).

A. THE WEAK PERFECTS.

64. This group comprises the perfects of the *i* and *a* conjugations as well as perfects in *-ei, -etti* and *-iedi*.

65. *The -ivi perfect.* The loss of *v* in the endings of the perfect dates back to Classical Latin times and even to early Latin, where a strong tendency to drop *v* between identical vowels is evident (cf. archaic Latin * *vivita* > CL *vita*). The loss of *v* in the perfect first affected the *-ire* conjugation where the required phonetic conditions for the elimination of *v* were present. Latin thus admits two collateral forms: *-ivi* and *-ii* (*partivi* and *partii*). The loss of *v* is generalized in the *-ivi* perfect and spreads from there to the *-avi* type as well.

partivi, partii > partii
partivisti > partisti
partivit > partì
*partivimus > partimus > * partimo > partimmo*
partivistis > partistis > partiste
CL *partivĕrunt > partivĕrunt > partirunt > partiro
    > partirono.*

THE PERFECT (Passato Remoto)

Preservation of the *-ivi* ending in the 1. pers. sing. is a Latinism, found in Brunetto Latini and used by Dante in rhyme. *Audivi* (with learned treatment of *au* as well) is found in Inf. 26, 78; other examples are found in the old poetic language where they reflect Sicilian usage. Rohlfs mentions a contracted form *parti*, used occasionally in the old language. It was probably never in common usage, since it failed to distinguish between the 1. and 3. pers. sing.

In the 2. pers. sing., the ending *-issi* (*-isi*) is encountered in the old dialects of the North: Old Lomb., Old Ven. *partissi*.

For the 3. pers. sing., Meyer-Lübke gives a Vulgar Latin form in *-iut*: CL *salīvit* > VL *saliut* > Old Italian *salio*. While a similar development appears quite normal for the *a* conjugation (*-avit* > *-aut*; cf. *avi-* as a secondary source for *au*: *avica* > *auca*), it is not easily explained on phonetic grounds in the case of *-ivit* where *v* should drop early. The Old Italian *-io* ending (*salio, partio*) is probably a direct analogy from *-áo* of the *a* conjugation (*cantavit* > *cantaut* > *cantáo*), and these all appear to be dialectal forms from the South. There are examples in Old Italian poetry: *morio, udio*, and in the Sicilian dialect: *muriu, partiu*. Due to the above-mentioned confusion between *partii* and *parti*, the *-io* ending is also carried into the 1. pers. sing.; Brunetto Latini has *uscio* (= *uscii*), and Dante, in Vita Nuova, uses *mi partio, mi sentio, io udio*. A contributing influence of the *-o* ending of the present indicative cannot be entirely excluded. Meyer-Lübke, considering *salio* the normal outcome, derives the modern form *salì* from an analogy with *cantò*, whereby both forms obtain a uniform oxytonic stress. This rather tenuous explanation is, on the whole, unacceptable, the more so as any such analogy with *cantò* would more likely have changed *salio* to *sagliò*. To sum up the explanation concerning *salio*: In the South, *cantaut* gives *cantáo*; *salio* is modeled after *cantáo* and is thus to be considered a Southern form.

In the 1. pers. plur., the gemination of *m* is not easily accounted for, since the preceding vowel is long (cf. *līma* > *lima*; *fūmu* > *fumo*). A compensatory lengthening of the consonant occurs after a short vowel: *hab(u)ĭmus* > *avemmo*, and *partimmo, cantammo* could then be analogical from such cases. Meyer-Lübke and Wiese are among the proponents of this theory. Rohlfs, on the other hand, explains the gemination as due to an assimilation of the cluster *vm* to *mm*, *v* having been reintroduced in an attempt to avoid confusion with the present tense (*cantavimus* > *cantamus* > *cantavmus > *cantammo*). However, a reappearance of *v* in this paradigm, be it for the sake of clarity, is not easily acceptable. Based on a similar type assimilation, yet avoiding the problem of a restoration of the *v*, is Grandgent's theory, according to which the origin of the gemination is to be found in the analogical influence of *dědĭmus* > * *dedmus* > *demmo*, and Rohlfs himself makes mention of the influence of *demmo* (*op. cit.* § 566). Lausberg (*op. cit.* § 824) suggests: *cantavimus* > *cantaimus > *cantammo*, in other words an assimilation of *i̯m* to *mm* (cf. *frĭgidu > **frei̯do* > *freddo*). The most plausible explanation appears to be an analogical influence of *demmo*.

In the 2. pers. plur., some Tuscan writers use an *-isti* ending, as does Machiavelli; these forms are criticized by 16th century grammarians.

In the 3. pers. plur., Latin had both *-ĕrunt* and *-'ĕrunt*; only the latter form survived. *Partiro* is common in Old Italian, but the loss of *n* in *partirunt* appears to be analogical rather than phonetic in view of the paroxytonic stress. It is brought about through influence from the strong perfect forms which have proparoxytonic stress: *scrípserunt* > *scrissero*. The subsequent addition of a *-no* ending is analogical from the present and the imperfect indicative (*partono, partivano*). The resulting combination of *-ro* + *-no* is not common in the South; Sicil. and Calabr. have *cantaru, moriru*, etc. Northern Italian *sentino* is based on syncopation and assimilation of the ending: *-irono* > * *-irno* > *-inno, -ino*. Dante has *apparinno* (Par. 14, 121), and *sentinno* is found in Old Lucchese. The strong flexion does not adopt the *-ro* +*-no* combination (*ebbero, fecero*), nor does the flexion in *-etti* (*credettero*).

66. *The -avi perfect.* The elimination of *v* is analogical from the *-ivi* group.

>   *cantavi* > *cantai*
>   *cantavisti* > *cantasti*
>   CL *cantavit* > VL * *cantaut* > *cantò*
>   *cantavimus* > *cantamus* > *cantammo*
>   *cantavistis* > *cantastis* > *cantaste*
>   *cantavĕrunt* > *cantarunt* > *cantaro* > *cantarono*

THE PERFECT *(Passato Remoto)*

The 1. pers. sing. ending *-ai* often becomes *-e* in the old dialects of the North; Old Piem. has *crié, trové*. There are a few occurrences of *-avi* in the South; it is a Latinized form just like *-ivi*.

In the 2. pers. sing., some dialects, especially those of the North, show the ending *-assi*: Old Lomb. *creassi*.

In Southern dialects, *-aut* gives *-áo, -áu*, a form which is encountered in Brunetto Latini and in the oldest lyrical poetry (*duráo, creáo*). At times, *-áo* is erroneously used in the 1. pers. sing. (*toccáo = toccai*), no doubt by analogy with the *-ivi* type where this particular confusion is more widespread, and of course also with some possible influence of the present indicative ending. Sicil. has *cantáu*, Calabr. has *mangiáu*, etc.

In the 2. pers. plur., Southern dialects have *cantasti* and sometimes add *vos* for the sake of clarity (S. Pugl. *cantástivu*).

The 3. pers. plur. ending in Old Italian is *-ro* (*cantaro, ordenaro*) to which *-no* is later added. A common ending in Old Tuscan is *-òrono* which has the stressed vowel of the 3. pers. sing.: *cantò* gives *cantòrono. Passòrono, montòrono* are found in Straparola; Dino Compagni has *chiamòrono, fermòrono*. Machiavelli uses the syncopated form *-orno*: *usorno, peccorno*. These forms also occur in Old Sienese and Old Pisan. The old form *-aro* has beside it a variant *-òro* which is used occasionally by Dante: *levorsi* (Inf. 26, 36 and 33, 60). By assimilation, *-orno* may give *-onno*; this form is attested for Old Pisan and Old Lucchese, and Dante offers an isolated example of it: *terminonno*. According to Rohlfs, *-onno* is still found in some modern dialects.

67. *The -ei perfect.* The *-ēre* conjugation, in by far most verbs, has a Latin perfect formation in *-ui*: *monēre - monui, tacēre - tacui, habēre - habui*. Cases of *-ēvi* are few: *delēre - delēvi, flēre - flēvi, complēre - complēvi*, and they do not constitute the origin of the *-ei* perfect. The *-ei* perfect is analogical from the *-ai* and *-ii* groups. The characteristic vowel *e* appears, through normal phonetic development, in the 2. pers. sing. and the 2. pers. plur.: *tĭm(u)ĭstī > temésti* and *tĭm(u)ĭstĭs > teméste*. This *e* is then generalized in a paradigm that follows the *-ai* and *-ii* pattern very closely. Both the *-ēre* and the *-ĕre* conjugations are affected by this formation, as shown by the verbs *temēre* and *crēdĕre*:

*teméi, temésti, temé, temémmo, teméste, temérono
credéi, credésti, credé, credémmo, credéste, credérono.*

Examples of this flexion are: *dovei, potei, godei.* Old Italian has *-éo* in the 3. pers. sing. by analogy with the Southern Italian development of * *cantaut* to *cantáo.* Examples are: *rendéo, potéo, rompéo.* As in the other conjugations, this ending may penetrate into the 1. pers. sing.; *io godéo* is found in Sacchetti. The Roman dialect has *-essi* instead of *-esti.* In the 3. pers. plur., Old Italian normally has *-ero* instead of *-erono*: *battero* (= *battèrono*). The syncopated and assimilated form (*-erono* > *-erno* > *-enno*) is found in Old Lucchese as well as in popular Tuscan (*potenno*). The *e* flexion merges with *i* in wide areas of Southern Italy: *perdii* = *perdèi*; *vinní* = *vendèi*.

Old Sienese *possei* (= *potei*) has adopted the thematic consonant of *posso* < *possum*.

68. *The -etti perfect.* Many *e* verbs use an analogical *-etti* ending which is derived from *detti,* itself analogical from *stetti* < * *stetui,* Vulgar Latin perfect of *stare.* The *-tt-* forms of the verb *stare* are limited to the 1. and 3. pers. sing. and the 3. pers. plur.: *stetti, stette, stettero*; the other forms are: *stesti, stemmo, steste.* Consequently, *-tt-* penetrates into the flexion of *dare* only in these same forms, following the pattern of its model; we thus get *detti, dette, dettero.*

Because of the existing parallelism between *desti, demmo, deste* on the one hand, and the corresponding forms of the *e* conjugation on the other, *-tt-* soon penetrated into the *e* verbs. The following analogies can be established: *desti : detti :: vendesti : x (vendetti); desti : dette :: vendesti - x (vendette); deste : dettero :: vendeste : x (vendettero).*

The first verbs to be affected by this change are those which are originally composita of *dare*: *perdere, rendere,* or which have *d* as a thematic consonant: *cadere, cedere,* but the *-etti* perfect soon acquires a wider extension. Dante has *tacetti, tacette,* and he even uses the *-etti* ending with *i* verbs: *seguette* (Par. 9, 141), *convenette* (Inf. 25, 42), *perseguette* (Purg. 22, 83). Perfects in *-etti* usually admit the traditional flexion in *-ei* as well: *credei - credetti, sedei - sedetti, dovei - dovetti.*

In certain dialects, -*etti* is used with verbs that have a strong perfect in Tuscan: Pisan *piacetti, nascetti, chiedetti*; Lucch. *scrivetti, vivetti, fetti* (= *feci*). The Lucchese dialect uses -*tt*- forms in the 1. pers. plur.: *credettimo, scrivettimo*; and Umbrian carries -*etti* into the *a* conjugation: *guardette* (= *guardò*), *cantette* (= *cantai*). *Andare* is influenced by *dare* of which it is often erroneously considered a compound; analogy with *detti* gives *andetti* which is encountered in popular Tuscan.

The ending of the 3. pers. plur. is usually -*ro*: *credettero, temettero,* and is seldom replaced by -*no*. *Tacettono* is found in Boccaccio. More widespread in Old Tuscan texts is a combination of -*ro* and -*no*: *pòtterono, stètterono*.

Carried into the *i* and *a* conjugations by analogy, -*etti* gives rise to the two analogical endings -*itti* and -*atti* which are encountered in the Lucchese dialect: *finitte, sentitte, pregatti, andatti, governatte*.

69. *The* -*iedi perfect.* The parallelism between *desti - vendesti, demmo - vendemmo,* etc., leads, in certain dialects (Sienese, Lucchese, popular Tuscan), to the creation of a new perfect ending -*iedi*: *vendiedi, rendiedi, perdiedi, andiedi, sentiedi*. The relationship between *dare* and *andare* may have touched off this development by creating an analogical *andiedi* (so Rohlfs, *op. cit.* § 579), but such a specific starting-point seems hardly necessary in this connection. Compare, for example, the success of this particular perfect formation in French. In fact, for Italian itself, D'Ovidio and Grandgent see in the -*ei* group, not a direct analogy from the -*ai* and -*ii* perfects, but a continuation of -*dĕdi* with the contrast in stress leveled out through analogy. Grandgent does add, however, that this flexion was later made to conform to the pattern of the -*ai* and -*ii* perfects.

B. THE STRONG PERFECTS

70. The strong perfect paradigm is not uniformly stressed, but consists of alternating strong and weak forms. The term "strong" refers to the forms that are accented on the root, while those that are stressed on the ending are referred to as "weak". Some changes occur in Vulgar Latin in the distribution of these forms: CL dixérunt > díxerunt, and CL díximus > VL dixímus. The perfect paradigm of dixi is given below as an illustration of accentuation in Classical and Vulgar Latin:

CL díxi > VL díxi
CL dixísti > VL dixísti
CL díxit > VL díxit
CL díximus > VL dixímus
CL dixístis > VL dixístis
CL dixérunt > VL díxerunt.

The 3. pers. plur. abandons CL -ĕrunt for -ĕrunt which existed in Latin along with the classical form. Dixímus has an analogical stress from dixístis; compare French where the analogy extends even further, changing -imes to -ismes. In some Italian dialects, the 1. pers. plur. is strong in conformity with its original accentuation: Lucch. díssimo, èbbimo, fècimo; Sicil. ábbimu, díssimu.

71. *Weak and strong roots.* A further differentiation between weak and strong forms comes about through the establishment of a distinctive weak root in the perfect: *feci - facesti, scrissi - scrivesti, dissi - dicesti,* etc. The model for this mixed flexion is probably to be sought in the *-ui* perfect where u disappears before a stressed ending, whereas, in the strong forms, it lengthens the preceding consonant. This gives the phonetic basis for the creation of a separate root in the weak forms: *tácui > tacqui - tac(u)ĭstī > tacesti;* * *cádui > caddi -* * *cad(u)ĭstī > cadesti.* In many verbs, this weak root happens to be identical with that of the present tense (compare here: *tacet > tace; cadit > cade*), and by analogy from such cases, the root of the present tense then spreads to other perfects: *scrīpsĭstī > scrivesti, dīxĭstī > dicesti,* etc. In addition, there may also be some general influence from the weak perfect group: *temi : temesti :: scrivi : x (scrivesti).*

72. *Dare and stare.* These are the only verbs with a strong perfect that do not have any weak forms (with the exception of *fui* which is strong throughout). We get *stetti - stesti* and not *stasti*. These verbs are rather isolated in that they do not contain the usual combination of stem vowel and stressed ending in the weak forms (cf. *feci - facésti*). *Stesti* and *desti* are preserved by analogy with

THE PERFECT (*Passato Remoto*)

the weak ending *-esti* as well as by the fact that a weak vowel cannot occur under the stress. Rohlfs, however, has attested the occurrence of *dasti* and *stasti* in Tuscan dialects of Lucca and Pistoia.

73. *The three strong perfect types.* The strong perfect comprises three main types: the *-ui* perfect, the sigmatic perfect and the ablaut perfect.

74. *The -ui perfect.* A number of *-ēre* verbs belong in this category: *tacēre - tacui, placēre - placui, habēre - habui, nocēre - nocui*, etc. There are many new creations in Vulgar Latin where the increasing popularity of the *-ui* perfect is directly related to the expansion of past participles in *-ūtum*. Participles in *-ūtum* call for an *-ui* perfect, just like *-ātum* corresponds to a perfect in *-ai* and *ītum* to a perfect in *-ii*. A couple of examples will serve to illustrate this process: CL *cadere* had a reduplication perfect, *cecĭdi*; in Vulgar Latin, it develops a past participle in *-ūtu,* * *cadūtu,* and the reduplication perfect is replaced by * *cadui*. *Bĭbĕre* has a Vulgar Latin past participle in *-ūtu*: * *bibūtu*; in the perfect, VL * *bibui* replaces CL *bibi*.

75. The phonetic development of consonant + u is not uniform in Italian: a) $k + u > kku$: k is lengthened, and u is kept; b) most other consonants are geminated, but u itself is lost; c) in a few cases, mainly following an l or an r, u becomes v, and there is no gemination.

76. $K + u > kku$: *tacui* > *tacqui*. The paradigm is as follows:

tacui > *tacqui*
tac(u)ĭstī > *tacesti*
tacuit > *tacque*
tac(u)ĭmus > *tacemmo*
tac(u)ĭstis > *taceste*
tácuĕrunt > *tacquero*.

Dialectal is 1. pers. sing. *io tacque*, used by Frezzi and Boiardo. The loss of *n* in the 3. pers. plur. is normal, due to the proparoxytonic accentuation, but *-no* may sometimes replace *-ro* in the old language. Dino Compagni has *misono, presono,* Sacchetti uses *ebbono, rimasono, feciono,* and Boccaccio has *dissono, trassono.*

Other verbs with a thematic *k* are: *plácui > piacqui, iacui > giacqui, nocui > nocqui.* CL *natus sum* is replaced by VL * *nacui > nacqui*; the weak forms of this verb have a thematic *sc* (*naścesti*) in agreement with the present stem infinitive *nascere*). The analogy behind the change to * *nacui* is not quite clear.

77. *Gemination of the thematic consonant and loss of ų: volui > volli.* This is by far the most common of the three groups of *-ui* perfects; it includes a large number of Vulgar Latin formations in addition to the Classical Latin verbs. In the examples below, the weak root is added in parenthesis:

> *tenui > tenni* (*tenesti*)
> CL *vēnī* > VL * *venui* (analogical from CL *tenui*) > *venni* (*venisti*)
> CL *stĕtī* > VL * *stetui* > *stetti* (no weak root, but sporadic occurrences of *stasti* in dialects)
> CL *cecĭdī* > VL * *cadui* > *caddi* (*cadesti*)
> CL *rūpī* > VL * *rūpuī* > *ruppi* (*rompesti*)
> CL *cognōvī* > VL * *co(g)novui* > *conobbi* (*conoscesti*).

VL * *conovui* > *conobbi* shows the normal phonological development of *v* + *ų* > *bb*; compare also CL *crēvī* > VL * *crevui* > *crebbi*. But some verbs have *v* + *ų* > *vv*, probably under analogical influence from the present tense, a form which is evident also in the weak root of the perfect. CL *bibi* > VL * *bĭbui* > *bevvi* (*bevesti*). *Bevvi* reveals influence from *beve* < *bĭbit*, or else it results from an analogy like: *cadesti* : *caddi* : : *bevesti* : *x* (*bevvi*). The Old Sienese dialect has *bebbi*. Another example is CL *plū(v)it* > VL * *plovuit* > *piovve* with influence from the pres. ind. *piove*; cf. Old Sienese *piobbe*.

78. *The passato remoto of avere and sapere.*

> *habui* > Old Tuscan, Old Umbrian, Old Roman *abbi*
> *sapui* > Old Roman *sappi.*

Modern Italian *ebbi* requires as etymology a form * *hēbuī* which could be analogical from *dēbui,* * *stĕtui*. In addition, Rohlfs (*op. cit.*

THE PERFECT *(Passato Remoto)* 69

§ 584) also suggests a possible influence from Northern Italy where a process of umlaut gives us Old Lomb. *heve* < * *habi*. The vocalic ablaut *e:a* in *feci - facesti* could possibly also have played a role in the creation of *ebbi*. A short form *ei* (= *ebbi*) is found in Old Tuscan and is used, for example, by Dante: *ei posato* (Inf. 1, 28). It is this short form that is used in the formation of the conditional: *temerei, partirei*.

The dialect of Rome has *ebbe* in the 1. pers. sing. Forms that have *i* in the stem (*ibbi, ibbe*) are common in Le Marche and other Southern regions. Sicilian has *appi, avisti*, with *appi* being analogical from *sappi* < *sapui*.

Modern Italian has *seppi* from *sapui*; the problem concerning the change to *e* in the stem is parallel to the development of *habui* to *ebbi*. *Seppi* is drawn from *ebbi*, and in some dialects, the close morphological relationship between *qvere* and *sapere* will also affect the consonant: Calabr. *eppi* (= *ebbi*), Sicil. *appi* (= *ebbi*).

79. *Dialectal perfects in -ui.* Other *-ui* type perfects are found in the various dialects of Italy. *Potti* < *potui* is encountered in Old Italian texts as well as in the Sicilian and Calabrian dialects; it is replaced, in Italian, by a regular weak formation in *-ei*. Dante has *viddi* < * *vidui* (Inf. 7, 20); Sacchetti uses *vedde*. Sicil., Calabr. *vitti* may be analogical from *potti*. Rohlfs (*op. cit.* § 582) quotes numerous other dialectal forms.

80. $u > v$: *parvi, sparvi*, Old Italian *dolvi*. $R + u$ occurs in *parui > parvi*, and also *sparvi*, a compound of *parere*. The *r* is not doubled before u (compare the treatment of $r + i$ as opposed to most other consonants followed by i: *-ariu > -aio*, but *sīmia > scimmia*), and u itself becomes a full-fledged consonant *v*, but it disappears in the weak root: *parvi - paresti*. The *v* also appears in the Old Italian present participle *parvente*, used by Dante, as well as in the Modern Italian noun *parvenza*; cf. Old Provençal *parven* and *parvensa*.

D'Ovidio terms the perfects in *-vi* semi-learned. This seems, indeed, to be the case with *dolui >* Old Italian *dolvi*, as compared with the normal development of *volui* to *volli*. *Dolve* is found in Dante (Inf. 2, 51), and the form *dolfe* is also encountered in Old Italian. Modern Italian has a sigmatic perfect: *dolsi - dolesti*.

81. $S + u$. In this particular cluster, u is lost early and does not cause the doubling of the preceding s: *posui* > *posi*; *consuere* > Southern Italian *cósere*. Old Italian *puosi* points to a very early loss of u, since this permits the diphthongization of *o* in an open syllable. It is tempting to ascribe this early change to an influence of the sigmatic perfect with which *posui* > *posi* would automatically merge. Modern Italian *posi* reveals influence of the weak root (*ponesti*) as well as of the present indicative (*pone* < *ponit*). Conversely, Old Italian *rispuosi* (< *respōnsī*) is analogical from *puosi*; *rispose* and *rispuosero* are both encountered in Boccaccio.

82. *The passato remoto of essere. Fui* is strong throughout: *fui, fosti, fu, fummo, foste, furono*. The quantity of the *u* in *fŭī* is short in Classical Latin, although some scholars quote the form as *fūī*; a *u* is obtained through umlaut, caused by the final long *ī*, and this vowel then spreads to other forms. The distribution of *u* and *o* forms in this paradigm follows the division between strong and weak forms, if we take into consideration that the 1. pers. plur. was strong in Classical Latin. In the old language, there was a tendency to level out this vocalic difference, and older forms like *fusti, fuste, fòro, fuoro, fuorono* have all been attested. *Funno* (< *furno* < *furono*) is found in popular Tuscan.

83. *The sigmatic perfect*. This perfect formation is characterized by the letter *s* and derives its name from the Greek letter sigma; the group is made up of Latin perfects in *-si* and *-xi* as well as of numerous analogical developments in Vulgar Latin or later periods. The use of the present stem as a weak root (*scrissi - scrivesti*) is analogical from the *-ui* perfect.

Through regular phonetic development, *-xi* merges with *-si*; following a consonant, *x* is simplified to *s* (ex.: *iunxi* > *giunsi*), and in intervocalic position, $x > ss$ in the paradigms (ex.: *dīxī* > *dissi*).

Latin perfects in -si:

      rīsī > *risi*
      rasi > *rasi*
      mansi > *(ri)masi*
      arsi > *arsi*
      scrīpsi > *scrissi*
      rosi > *rosi*

THE PERFECT *(Passato Remoto)*

(in)clūsi > *chiusi*
persuasi > *persuasi*
mīsi > *misi*. The Sienese dialect has *messi*, analogical from the past participle *messo* < *mĭssu*. Sacchetti and Pulci have *missi* which represents some sort of a compromise between *misi* and *messi*.

Latin perfects in -xi:

planxi > *piansi*
finxi > *finsi*
pinxi > *pinsi*
strinxi > *strinsi*
iunxi > *giunsi*
dīxi > *dissi*
traxi > *trassi*
duxi > *dussi*
frīxi > *frissi*
coxi > *cossi.*

84. *Later analogical formations. Fransi* (CL *frēgi*) is drawn from *piansi*; *punsi* (CL *pupugi*) from *giunsi*; *vinsi* (CL *vīci*) from *finsi, pinsi*. A Vulgar Latin perfect * *lexi* (> *lessi*) replaces CL *lēgi*; some compounds of *legere* actually have a perfect in *-lexi* in Classical Latin: *dilexi, intellexi,* and combined with this is pressure from *regere*: *rego* : *rexi* : : *lego* : *x* (*lexi*). *Colsi, tolsi, dolsi, scelsi, uccisi* (CL *occīdi*), *intrisi* (CL *intrivi*) have all joined this group by analogy. *Mossi* (CL *mōvi*) is modeled on *scrissi* (cf. *muovere, scrivere*), *valsi* (CL *valui*) on *colsi, tolsi*.

Several verbs have a perfect in *-si* and a past participle in *-su(m)*: *risi - risu(m), rasi - rasu(m)*, etc. By analogy, verbs which have a past participle in *-su(m)* may develop a perfect in *-si*: *risu* : *risi* : : *fusu* : *x* (*fusi*); cf. CL *fudi*. Other examples of this process:

prehensu and VL *prehensi* > *presi* (CL *prehendi*)
accensu and VL *accensi* > *accesi* (CL *accendi*)
offensu and VL *offensi* > *offesi* (CL *offendi*)
responsu and VL *responsi* > *risposi* (CL *respondi*)
cŭrsu and VL *cŭrsi* > *corsi* (CL *cucurri*)
defensu and VL *defensi* > *difesi* (CL *defendi*)
morsu and VL *morsi* > *morsi* (CL *momordi*).

The infinitive constitutes an additional morphological agreement: *ridere* as compared with *prehendere, offendere*, etc. It is to be noted, in this connection, that CL *mordēre* had become *mórdĕre* in Vulgar Latin.

Analogy with *prehendere - presi* gives us the perfect *persi* for *perdere* and a past participle *perso* (CL *perdĭtum*) from *preso*. Similar analogies affect *tendere* and VL *rendere* (CL *reddere*), producing *tesi* and *teso* (CL *tetendi* and *tentum*), *resi* and *reso* (CL *reddĭdi* and *reddĭtum*). For *abscondere*, we get *ascosi* and *ascoso*.

Alongside with *parvi*, Modern Italian also admits a sigmatic *parsi* which may have been influenced by *dolsi* (CL *parui, dolui*); *apersi* then comes from *parsi*. *Offerre*, which has an analogical infinitive *offrire* from *aprire*, also acquires a sigmatic perfect: *offersi*.

Some of the sigmatic perfects admit a collateral weak form in Modern Italian: *apersi - aprii, offersi - offrii, persi - perdei* and *perdetti, resi - rendei* and *rendetti*.

Old Italian writers use many sigmatic perfects that have not been continued in Modern Italian, and some of these forms are kept in the dialects. Dante, Petrarca and Straparola use *vólsi*, and Pulci has *volsero*. *Volsi* is still found in the dialects of Pistoia, Lucca and Pisa. *Salsi* is found in Petrarca. Popular Tuscan has *vensi, viensi* (= *venni*); and *tensi, tiensi* (= *tenni*) occur in the dialects of Lucca, Pisa and Livorno.

85. *The ablaut perfect.* In Latin, some verbs form a perfect stem through a process of ablaut (or apophony) of the stem vowel:

>   *facio - fēci*
>   *vĭdeo - vīdi*
>   *mĭtto - mīsi*
>   *rŭmpo - rūpi*
>   *stare - stĕti.*

For Italian, the ablaut phenomenon can be observed within the perfect paradigm itself, since the weak root of the verb is that of the present tense:

>   *feci - facesti*
>   *vidi - vedesti*
>   *misi - mettesti*
>   *ruppi - rompesti.*

THE PERFECT *(Passato Remoto)*

Avere and *sapere* may have acquired their ablaut perfect by analogy with this verb group, with *ebbi - avesti* and *seppi - sapesti* modeled on *feci - facesti*.

Sicil., Calabr. *vitti* (= *vidi*) is drawn from *potti* or *detti*. *Desti* yields a short form *dei*, possibly through the influence of *credesti - credei*, and this analogy spreads to other verbs: *stei, fei, ei*. *Denno, stenno* and *fenno* are analogical from such forms as *funno, fanno*.

86. *The reduplication perfects: stĕti and dĕdi.* The so-called reduplication perfects of Classical Latin are related to the ablaut perfects, since the stem is normally repeated in ablaut form:

> *cadere - cecidi*
> *tangere - tetigi*
> *pungere - pupugi*
> *parcere - peperci*
> *canere - cecini.*

Not much remains of this rather complicated perfect formation. *Stĕti* had become **stĕtui* in Vulgar Latin, and *dĕdi* may therefore be considered the only survivor. In the case of *stare*, there are a few sporadic occurrences of the original *e - a* ablaut: *stetti - stasti*. *Dare*, as is to be expected, follows *stare* closely with dialectal instances of the *e - a* ablaut; the Calabrian dialect, for example, has *detti - dasti*. But in addition, *dĕdi* has achieved a new secondary ablaut through diphthongization of the strong root as opposed to non-diphthongization of the weak root: *diedi - desti*. *Detti*, analogical from *stetti*, levels out this apophony. We get the following perfect paradigm of *dare*:

> *diedi - detti*
> *desti*
> *diede (diè) - dette*
> *demmo*
> *deste*
> *diedero - dettero.*

The reduction of *diede* to *diè* is normal; cf. *piede > piè*.

THE PAST PARTICIPLE

87. The past participles, like the perfects, are either weak (stressed on the ending) or strong (accented on the root).

A. THE WEAK PAST PARTICIPLES

88. *-atu* > *-ato*. This is the regular ending of the past participle of the *a* conjugation. Examples:

laudatu > *lodato*
portatu > *portato*
cantatu > *cantato*.

The *-ato* ending also spreads to *-are* verbs which have a strong past participle in Classical Latin:

crepāre	CL *crepĭtum*	Italian *crepato*
cŭbāre	CL *cubĭtum*	Italian *covato*
domāre	CL *domĭtum*	Italian *domato*
vĕtāre	CL *vetĭtum*	Italian *vietato*
secāre	CL *sectum*	Italian *segato*
iŭvāre	CL *iūtum*	Italian *giovato*
sonāre		Italian *sonato*
tonāre		Italian *tonato*.

Sonare has no past participle in Classical Latin; the same is true for *tonare*, but compare CL *attonĭtum*.

Southern dialects have an *-atu* ending: *portatu, cantatu*. Northern dialects have a variety of forms: *-ado* (ex. Old Lomb. *formado*), *-ao* (ex.: Old Ligur. *dao*), *-á* (ex.: Lomb. *cantá*), *-ò* (ex.: Ticin.

THE PAST PARTICIPLE 75

lavò). Rohlfs (*op. cit.* § 620) gives a large number of other dialectal forms.

89. -*ītu* > -*ito*. This is the regular past participle of the *i* conjugation. Examples:

> *finitu* > *finito*
> *partitu* > *partito*
> *auditu* > *udito*.

The dialectal endings are parallel to the ones outlined for -*ato*: -*itu* in the South, in the North -*ido, -io, -i*.

90. -*ūtu* > -*uto*. In Classical Latin, only verbs in -*uĕre* had a past participle in -*ūtum*, as shown in the examples below (the verbs are listed in the infinitive, the perfect and the past participle):

> *minuĕre*   *minui*   *minūtum*
> *statuĕre*   *statui*   *statūtum*
> *constituĕre* *constitui*   *constitūtum*
> *tribuĕre*   *tribui*   *tribūtum*.

From these few cases, -*utu* was widely extended in Vulgar Latin where it came to be used in a great many verbs having a perfect in -*ui*. And in Italian, it has spread to the point where it represents the normal weak participle of the *e* conjugation, thus forming a parallel to -*ato* and -*ito*. Rohlfs (*op. cit.* § 622) seems to believe that it first spread from -*uĕre* to the -*ĕre* conjugation in general, and then, by analogy, to the -*ēre* group, this latter transition being facilitated by the coexistence of a few -*ĕre* and -*ēre* forms (*fulgĕre* - *fulgēre*, *stridĕre* - *stridēre*), as well as by frequent changes in Vulgar Latin from the one group to the other. But its spread would seem to be more directly related to the extension of the -*ui* perfect than to the nature of the infinitive.

Dialectal endings are -*utu* in the South; the North has a set of endings with alternate forms in *u* and *ü*: -*udo, -üdo, -uo, -üo, -u, -ü*.

Following are examples of *e* conjugation verbs with an analogical Vulgar Latin past participle in -*utu*:

> CL *habēre, habui, habĭtum*, VL * (*h*)*abūtu* > *avuto*.
> The form *aúto* is attested for Old Sienese; it reflects the

tendency of *v* to drop before *u* and *o* (cf. *pavōre* > *paura*). Tuscan, however, retains *v* in agreement with the infinitive root *av-ere*.

CL *vĭdēre, vīdī, vīsum*. Old Italian *viddi* goes back to a Vulgar Latin perfect **vidui* which, in turn, yields the analogical past participle **vĭdūtu* > *veduto*. The tendency of pretonic *e* to go to *i* is obstructed within the paradigms by a strong analogical influence from the stem-stressed forms (*vedi, vede*, etc.). Modern Italian also has the participle *visto*, from VL **vīsĭtu*, analogical from *pósĭtu* > *posto*. The *ī* comes from CL *vīsum*.

CL *debēre, debui, debĭtum*. VL **debūtu* > *dovuto*.

CL *valēre, valui*. VL **valūtu* > *valuto*. Old Tuscan *vagliuto* has the palatalized stem of the 1. pers. sing. of the pres. ind. and of the pres. subj. (Old Italian *vaglio, vaglia*). Modern Italian also has *valso*, analogical from the sigmatic perfect *valsi*.

CL *tenēre, tenui*. VL **tenūtu* > *tenuto*. There are cases of a palatalized root in Old Italian; Girardo Patecchio has *tegnudo*.

VL *sapēre, sapui*. VL **sapūtu* > *saputo*.

VL *volēre*, CL *volui*. VL **volūtu* > *voluto*. A palatalized root is found in Cors. *vugliutu*.

VL *potēre*, CL *potui*. VL **potūtu* > *potuto*. *Possuto*, built on *posso*, is fairly common in Tuscan dialects. Venetian has *posudo*; Bonvesin uses *possuo*.

CL *iacēre, iacui*. *Giaciuto*, from VL **iacūtu*, is built on the present stem (inf. *giacere*).

CL *nocēre, nocui, nocĭtum*. VL **nocūtu* > *nociuto*, with the present stem being used to form the Italian participle (inf. *nuocere*).

VL *cadēre*, CL *cecīdi*, VL **cadui*. VL **cadūtu* > *caduto*.

CL *sedēre, sēdi, sessum*. VL **sedūtu* > *seduto*.

CL *vendĕre* (*perdĕre, credĕre*, etc.), *vendĭdi, vendĭtum*. VL **vendūtu* > *venduto*. *Perdere*, in addition, has a participle *perso* analogical from a sigmatic perfect *persi*.

CL *complēre, complēvi, complētum*. VL **complūtu* > *compiuto*. The past participle *compito* is derived from the infinitive *compire*, collateral form of *cómpiere*.

CL *bĭbĕre, bībi*, (*pōtum*). VL **bĭbui* and **bĭbūtu* > *bevuto*.

CL *plŭĕre, plū(v)it*. *Piovuto* is based on *piove, piovere*, going back to forms in *ŏ* (cf. VL **plŏia* > *pioggia* and French *pluie*).

CL *vīvĕre, vīxi*. The perfect stem is used in the formation of the past participle *vissuto* < VL **vīxūtu*; this development may have been prompted by a VL perfect *vīxui > vissi.

91. *Other participles in -uto.* Tuscan dialects present various cases of participles in *-uto* built on a sigmatic form: *volsuto, vensuto, valsuto*. Dialectal examples of a participle in *-uto*, corresponding to a strong form in Tuscan, are not uncommon: Lucch. *leggiuto, nasciuto, renduto*, etc. In other cases, Tuscan itself admits both a strong and a weak participle: *perso - perduto, fesso - fenduto, cesso - ceduto, cotto - cociuto, valso - valuto, visto - veduto*. *Paruto* (= *parso*) is common in older Tuscan.

92. *The past participle of essere - stare.* Old Italian *essuto*, used by Brunetto Latini and Machiavelli, is derived from the infinitive root *ess-ere*. A shortened form, *suto*, is used by Brunetto Latini, Cecco Angiolieri, Guittone, Dino Compagni, Boccaccio; it constitutes another example of the alternance between *es-* and *s-* forms in this verb (cf. *ĕs > *sĕs > sei; estis > *sĕtis > siete*). Modern Italian has no participle of *essere*; it is replaced by *stato* from *stare*.

93. *Cases of -uto in the i conjugation.* The penetration of *-uto* into the *i* conjugation affects the verb *venire* where the past participle *venuto* is analogical from *tenuto*, but Old Tuscan yields numerous examples that are not based on any such precise analogy: *falluto, finuto, pentuto, vestuto, sentuto, servuto*, etc. It is a very common feature, shared also by Old French (cf. Old French *partu, sentu, repentu, faillu, remplu*). The *-uto* participle is particularly frequent in Southern dialects where *-ere* and *-ire* verbs tend to merge, since *e* and *i* both give *i*.

94. *Shortened participles or verbal adjectives.* The shortening in Tuscan of past participles in *-ato* to *-ó* (ex.: *trovato > trovo*) may have been caused by the coexistence of Classical Latin and Vulgar Latin participles, such as *ausum (> oso) - *ausatu (> osato), ūsum (> uso) - *usatu (> usato), tractum (> tratto) - *tractatu (> trattato)*, etc. Other participles in *-atus* have, beside them, an adjective or a noun in *-us*: *albatus - albus*. *Oso, albo*, etc., then came to be considered abridged forms of *osato, albato*, and thus served as a model for the syncopation of other *-ato* participles in Tuscan. From Tuscany, the verbal adjectives spread to other regions of Italy. Examples of this construction:

> è tocco lo meridian dal sole (Purg. 4, 137)
> noi avemo guasto tutto Cholle (Lettera Senese del 1260; (Mon. 74, 118).

B. THE STRONG PAST PARTICIPLES

95. *Participles in -sum.* The Latin participles in *-sum* are normally retained in Italian (> *-so*). These participles originated in Latin from various sources.

From *d* or *t* + *s*:

> mĭttere - mĭssu > messo
> VL rídere - rīsu > riso
> VL árdere - VL arsu > arso
> cedere - cessu > cesso (and also a weak form *ceduto*)
> accendere - accensu > acceso
> (in)clūděre - (in)clūsu > chiuso
> defendere - defensu > difeso
> divīděre - divīsu > diviso
> fŭnděre - fūsu > fuso
> evaděre - VL evasu > evaso
> invaděre - VL invasu > invaso
> VL mórdere - morsu > morso
> offendere - offensu > offeso
> prehendere - prehensu > preso
> descendere - descensu > disceso, sceso.

From verbs in *-rgěre*:

> mergere - mersu > merso, immerso
> tergere - tersu > terso
> spargere - sparsu > sparso.

From a few verbs with other thematic consonants (*r, n, m,* etc.):

> cŭrrěre - cŭrsu > corso
> remanēre - remansu > rimaso (*rimasto* is analogical from *posto*)
> oppriměre - oppressu > oppresso.

THE PAST PARTICIPLE

The parallelism which exists in many verbs between a past participle in *-so* and a sigmatic perfect (ex.: *riso* - *risi*) is instrumental in a further extension of this group: *valso, parso, perso* (cf. CL *perdĭtum*), *reso* (cf. CL *reddĭtu*), etc. *Mosso* is based on VL *mossi* (cf. CL *mōvī*), itself analogical from *scrissi* (inf. *muovere* - *scrivere*), or perhaps from *pressi* - *presso* with which it is related in meaning.

From *abscondere* is developed a Vulgar Latin participle *absco(n)su* (cf. CL *abscondĭtum*) > *ascoso*. *Nascoso* is from **inabsco(n)su*; *nascosto* shows influence of *posto*.

CL *fīxu* > *fisso* becomes *fiso* by analogy with other participles in *-iso*, the ending *-isso* being an isolated form in the past participle. Modern Italian *fitto* is from *fīctu*, collateral form of *fīxu* in Classical Latin.

96. *Old Tuscan past participles in -so.* *Cosso* is analogical from the perfect *cossi*. Modern Italian has a weak participle, *cociuto*, and the Classical Latin participle *cŏctu* gives *cotto* which is also retained. *Visso* is analogical from *vissi*; modern Italian has *vissuto*. *Resso* is based on *ressi*; modern Italian *retto* is from CL *rēctum*. *Dolso* is from *dolsi* and is replaced, in Modern Italian, by a weak participle *doluto*.

The influence of the perfect may, at times, extend to the thematic vowel. Old Italian *miso*, Lucch. and Pisan *misso* show analogical influence of *mīsī* on *mĭssu*. Compare dialectal *ditto* for *detto*.

97. *Participles in -tum.* Participles in *-tum* are mainly found in *-ĕre* verbs, having *c* or *g* as a thematic consonant, but there are other cases besides.

Examples with *c* and *g*:

> *regere* - *rēctu* > *retto*
> *legere* - *lēctu* > *letto*
> *fingere* - *fīctu* > *fitto*
> *afflīgere* - *afflīctu* > *afflitto*
> *trahere*, VL **tragere* - *tractu* > *tratto*
> *facere* - *factu* > *fatto*
> *dīcere* - *dĭctu* > *detto*. Lucch., Pisan *ditto* shows influence
>   of the perfect *dīxī*; cf. French *dit*.

dūcere - dŭctu > dotto
iŭngere - iŭnctu > giunto
plangere - planctu > pianto.

Examples with other thematic consonants:

scrībere - scriptu > scritto
morī - mortuu, VL mortu > morto
aperire - apertu > aperto
cooperire - copertu > coperto
nascī - natu > nato
sepelire - sepŭltu > sepolto.
capere - captu > Old Italian catto. This form is used by Dante.

98. *Restoration of the n infix.* Many Latin verbs show an alternance of forms with or without *n*: *frangere, frango, frēgi, fractum*; *pingere, pingo, pinxi, pictum*; **vincere, vinco, vīci, victum.** CL *fractu* as compared with Italian *franto* shows restoration in the past participle of the *n* infix of *frango* and *frangere*. Other examples are: *fingere - fictu > finto, pingere - pictu > pinto, vincere - victu > vinto*. This particular restoration process lacks consistency, nor is there any obvious reason why Latin has *pictum* and *cinctum*. Compare *pinto* with the noun *pittore* and compare French *peintre*.

99. *Analogical formations in -to. Collēctu* should give *colletto*, a form attested for Old Italian, and which has survived in the noun *colletta*, but is otherwise replaced by *colto*. In the same fashion, * *ex-electu* should give * *sceletto*, and we should expect the following developments: *erectu* > * *eretto, porrectu* > * *porretto, sorrectu* > * *sorretto*. In all these participles, the stress moves forward to the initial syllable by analogy with the present and the infinitive (cf. *colgo, cogliere*), and the weak vowel is then syncopated: *colto, scelto, erto, porto, sorto*. A further analogy could come from the sigmatic perfects that have a past participle in *-to*: *piansi : pianto :: sorsi : x (sorto)*.

An analogical *tolletto* is attested in Dante (Par. 5, 33); cf. Old French *toleit, toloit*. CL *sublatu* is replaced by VL * *tollĭtu* on the basis of an analogy with the *-ĕre* group in general (*credĭtu, perdĭtu, vendĭtu*, etc.). *Tolto* is obtained through syncopation of the weak vowel. Similar instances are: CL *volūtu* > VL * *volvĭtu* > *volto*;

THE PAST PARTICIPLE 81

CL *solūtu* > VL *solvĭtu* > *solto*; VL *dolĭtu* > Old Italian *dolto*, but Modern Italian *doluto*.

Non-syncopated forms are *débito* and *lécito*, both learned in nature; other non-syncopated participles are encountered in the dialects.

Offerto and *sofferto* are based on *aperto*.

Vīxu, analogical from *vīxī*, gives Old Italian *visso*. It is replaced by *vissuto*, built on the perfect stem in spite of being a weak form. There are Northern Italian examples of *vivuto*.

Dante uses *ricetto* < *receptu*, later replaced by a weak participle: *ricevuto*. *Redento* (< *redemptu*) and *assunto* (< *ad-sumptu*) are learned.

100. *Strong past participles in -sto.* *Posĭtu* > *posto* is the only example in Classical Latin, but early Vulgar Latin had * *vīsĭtu* > *visto* (cf. Spanish *visto*) and * *quaesĭtu* > *chiesto*, all with syncopation of the weak vowel between *s* and *t*. By analogy with these few, but common verbs, other participles in -*sto* are created: *nascoso - nascosto, rimaso - rimasto, risposo - risposto*. There are additional cases in the dialects: *chiusto* (= *chiuso*), *mosto* (= *mosso*), etc.

THE GERUND AND THE PRESENT PARTICIPLE

101. *The gerund.* The endings of the gerund in Latin are: 1. *-ando* (ex.: *laudando*), 2. - 3. *-endo* (ex.: *monendo, agendo*), 4. *-iendo* (ex.: *audiendo*). The only major change occurs in the fourth conjugation, where *-iendo* is replaced by *-endo*; this leaves Italian with two gerund endings: *-ando* in the *a* conjugation, *-endo* elsewhere. Examples:

1. *laudando* > *lodando*
2. *temendo* > *temendo*
3. *credendo* > *credendo*
4. *partiendo* > *partendo*.

In Northern dialects, *-ando* may penetrate into the other conjugations: Old Gen. *ferando, odando, combatando*; Piem. *vedand, savand*. In certain Southern dialects, *-endo* may replace *-ando*: Roman *parlènno, lavènno,* and in Northern Italy, there are rare cases of *-indo*: Piem. *drumint* (= *dormendo*). Rohlfs (*op. cit.* § 618) has a wealth of dialectal examples of these changes.

Old Italian *veggiendo* and *vogliendo* are based on the stem of the present tense (*veggio, voglio*). This same analogy appears also in the present participle.

102. *The present participle.* The Latin endings are: 1. *-ante* (ex.: *laudante*), 2. - 3. *-ente* (ex.: *monente, agente*), 4. *-iente* (ex.: *audiente*). Of these endings, *-ante* and *-ente* are kept, but little remains of *-iente*. The present participle has lost its verbal character in Italian, words of this category having become adjectives or nouns. Examples:

1. *laudante* > *lodante*
2. *temente* > *temente*
3. *credente* > *credente*
4. *partiente* > *partente*.

Examples of *-iente*:

nutrire - *nutriente*
ubbidire - *ubbidiente*
sentire - *sentiente*
salire - *saliente*
venire - *veniente*
dormire - *dormiente* or *dormente*
sapere - *sapiente*. This is an *e* verb, but an analogy could occur in the 1. pers. sing. of the pres. ind.; cf. *sapẹo* and *sentịo*.

Old Tuscan has *vegnente* and *vogliente* with the palatalized root of the 1. pers. sing. of the pres. ind. *Sacciente* (*saccente*) is termed a "gallicismo" by D'Ovidio, but may also have come in from the South where we find *saccio*. Another example with a palatalized root is *veggente*, related to Old Italian *veggio* < *vĭdeo*. *Parvente* and *valsente* are analogical from the root of the perfect.

Wide regions of Italy use *-ente* for *-ante*: Lucch., Pist. *tirente, trionfente*; Old Sienese *lavorente*; Old Ligur. *parlente, pesente*. The opposite substitution is rare: Ven. *bevante*.

THE FUTURE

103. The synthetic future of Classical Latin (*amabo*, etc.) is replaced in Romance by an analytical periphrasis, consisting of the infinitive followed by the present tense of an auxiliary verb which, in most areas of Romania, is *habere* (ex.: *scrībĕre habeo, vĕnīre habet*). This construction originally expressed obligation, *habeo* being more or less the equivalent of *debeo*, but it soon became the normal formula of futurity.

When used as future endings, the forms of the present tense of *habere* are reduced in the 1. and 2. pers. plur. where the *ab-* portion is dropped. The future of *cantare* is given as an example of this formation:

* *cantare aio* > *canterò*
* *cantare as* > *canterai*
* *cantare at* > *canterà*
* *cantare (hab)emus* > *canteremo*
* *cantare (hab)etis* > *canterete*
* *cantare habent* > *canteranno*.

The stress pattern in the infinitive changes radically with the addition of a stressed ending. This places the characteristic vowel of the infinitive in a very weak position between initial and main stress (ex.: *pártirò*), and this particular circumstance has had a direct influence on the *-are* group, changing *a* to *e* before *r* in the weak intertonic position, a common phonetic feature in Italian as well as in Romance in general (cf. VL *seperare, comperare*; Italian *lazzeretto*, derived from *Lazaru*). It also accounts for the creation of various syncopated forms (ex.: *vedrò, vorrò, potrò*). Old Sienese keeps the *a* (ex.: *cantarò*) and even uses it in the other conjugations, too (ex.: *mettarò, perdarò*). The final unstressed *e* of the infinitive is dropped before the stressed ending.

The 1. pers. sing. of the present tense of *habere* shows a variety of phonological developments in Old and dialectal Italian, as shown in § 39, and these various forms also appear as future endings. Besides the usual ending -*ò*, Old Tuscan has -*aggio*: *faraggio* is found in Cecco Angiolieri (Mon. 169, III, 10), *faragio* in Giacomo da Lentino (Mon. 41, V, 148) and Compagnetto da Prato (Mon. 58, I, 2). The -*agio* ending is common in the Old Sienese dialect which also has -*abbo*: *dirabbo, metterabbo*. Tommaso da Faenza has *farabo* (Mon. 109, 48), and *dirabo* is found in Compagnetto da Prato (Mon. 58, I, 25). Another future ending is -*aço*; *vederaço* and *perderaço* are found in the Laude (Mon. 159, VIII, 4-5), and this same text has *veço* for *vedo*. Southern dialects have -*aio* or -*agiu*: *faraio* (Mon. 26, 84), *daraio* (Mon. 140, 78), *diraio* (Mon. 161, 179); Northern dialects have -*ai* and -*è*: Old Ven., Old Lomb. *farai*; Old Pad. *farè*.

Cases of epenthesis are fairly common in Old Italian; *avroe* and *daroe* are found in the Romanzo di Tristano (Mon. 130, 133; ib. 114). This epenthesis also occurs in the 3. pers. sing.: *sarae* (Mon. 30, 54), and, in the same text (Breve di Montieri): *darae* (35), *avarae* (57 and 60), *verrae* (103).

The 1. pers. plur. drops the *av-*, but otherwise retains the Old Italian present of the auxiliary (*av-emo*) as a future ending, whereas the verb itself adopts the subjunctive form *abbiamo*. The older language sometimes replaces -*emo* by -*eno* (for a similar development, see -*iano* for -*iamo*); Macchiavelli has: *vorreno, verreno, sareno*.

104. *Syncopated forms.* In a few verbs, the weak vowel of the infinitive is syncopated in the future tense. The thematic consonant is usually *t, d, p, b* or *r* (before another *r*); the resulting cluster of consonants is thus a familiar one and easy to pronounce. If the thematic consonant is *l* or *n*, it is assimilated to the following *r*.

The thematic consonant is *t, d, p* or *b*:

  potēre - potrò
  cadēre - cadrò
  debēre - dovrò

sapēre - saprò
vĭdēre - vedrò
habēre - avrò
audīre - udrò (or *udirò*).

The thematic consonant is *r*:

* *morīre - morrò* (or *morirò*)
parēre - parrò.

The thematic consonant is *n* or *l*:

tenēre - terrò
valēre - varrò
venīre - verrò
volēre - vorrò
dolēre - dorrò (but *solere - solerò*).

Syncopation after *r* was more widespread in Old Italian: *perseverrò, adoperrà*, etc., and -*rr*- is sometimes falsely used by analogy with such cases; Machiavelli has *troverreno*, Straparola has *arrai*. Metathesis of *r* may occur in the future tense: *entrerò* > *enterrò*, a form encountered in Boccaccio. This same phenomenon can be observed in Old French futures: *duerrai* (= *durerai*), *enterra* (= *entrera*).

The Lucchese dialect has several non-syncopated forms: *caderò, venirò, morirò*, etc.

105. *Darò, starò, farò*. No weakening of *a* to *e* could occur in the future of these verbs, since *a* is not intertonic. *Sarò* is analogical from this group; it replaces Old Italian *serò* < * *(es)sere aio*, and this change also affects the conditional: Old Italian *serebbe* > *sarebbe*. Old Italian *arò* (= *avrò*), used by Machiavelli, is modeled on *sarò, darò*; cf. Old French *arai*.

D'Ovidio quotes a syncopated form *drò* (= *darò*) from Albertano di Brescia, and *frò* (= *farò*) from Buonarroti.

106. *Ero, fiam*. Old Northern Italian texts occasionally use the old Latin future *ero*, which is also kept in Old French and Old Provençal. Monaci (60, I, 54), has an example from Girardo Patecchio of *er* < *ĕrit*: *er mateça tegnua*.

Old Tuscan has sporadic examples of *fia, fie* (= *sarà*) and *fiano, fieno* (= *saranno*), used by Dante, Boccaccio and Machiavelli; the etymology is *fiam*, etc. These forms are also encountered in the Novellino (Mon. 154, 116-117): *Lo 'mperio fia ora più volte mutato, le genti fiano ora tutte nuove; dove ritornerei?*

Firà, future of *fir* < *fieri*, is found in Uguccione da Lodi (Mon. 62, 121): *En un celicio firà 'l corpo metuo*. Barsegapé has: *clamao firà* (= *sarà chiamato*).

107. *Separable futures.* Old Northern as well as Southern dialects sometimes kept the infinitive and the auxiliary separated in conformity with the analytical origin of the future tense. Most often, the auxiliary precedes: *a portare* (= *porterà*); Barsegapé has: *turbar se n'a lo sol*. The same construction is also found in Old Sardinian where it occurs, for example, in the Privilegio Logudorese; *aet potestare, aem levare, aet exere.*

THE CONDITIONAL

108. This tense is a new creation in Romance, a past future formed from the infinitive combined with a past tense of the auxiliary.

109. *The habui type.* Tuscan forms its conditional with *habui* instead of *habebam* which is the most common formation elsewhere in Romania, including vast regions of Italy itself. The conditional endings are thus, in Tuscan, derived from the perfect of *habere*.

* cantare habui > Old Italian canterebbi > canterei
* cantare habuisti > canteresti
* cantare habuit > canterebbe
* cantare habuimus > canteremmo
* cantare habuistis > cantereste
* cantare habuerunt > canterebbero.

In the 1. pers. sing., the Old Tuscan (and Old Umbrian, Old Roman) form *abbi* (< *habui*) does not appear to have been commonly used as a conditional ending. Grandgent mentions this form, however, and even goes as far as to derive *-ebbi* from a cross between *-abbi* and *-ei*. In Old Italian, the 1. pers. sing. ends in *-ebbi*; Guittone has *vivrebbi*. Old Tuscan also had a short form *ei* (= *ebbi*) of the auxiliary; cf. *ei posato* (Inf. 1, 28). But the conditional ending *-ei* is more likely derived from an analogy with the passato remoto of the *e* conjugation: *temesti : canteresti, tememmo : canteremmo :: temei : x (canterei)*. The existence of 3. pers. sing. forms in *-è* (*cantarè*, analogical from *temè*) makes this latter explanation even more plausible. Pulci has *potrè*, Buonarroti *darè*.

The old dialects of the North often have *-ev, -ef* or *-avi, -ovi*: Old Berg. *voref* (= *vorrei*), Old Lomb. *trovaraf* (= *troverebbe*), Old Ven. *poravi* (= *porrei*), etc. Guido Fava has *serave, sareve, podrave* in the 3. pers. sing., and *podrave, sapravi* in the 1. pers. sing. (Mon. 33 and 34).

In the 1. pers. plur., an analogical *-essimo* ending is sometimes used. It owes its origin to a close relationship with some endings of the imperfect subjunctive as well as to a certain modal affinity in the irrealis type of conditional clauses. *Aveste : avessimo :: avreste : x (avressimo)*. These forms are found in Ariosto (*avressimo, anderessimo*), and Trissino lists them in his paradigm of the conditional. Straparola has *averessimo*, Verri *dovressimo*, Alfieri *potressimo*.

In the 3. pers. plur., the endings are *-ebbero* or, at times, *-ebbono*, in agreement with the usual fluctuation in the 3. pers. plur. of the perfect.

110. *The habebam type.* Most areas of Romania use the imperfect of *habere* (*cantare habebam*) in the formation of the conditional, and this type is also fairly common in Old Italian.

Habebam > *avea*, with elimination of one *b* by dissimilation; *cantare avea* should then, after the usual omission of *av-*, give *cantarea*. This form has been attested, but is essentially dialectal, characteristic of Arezzo and of some Northern dialects. Examples: *farea* (Bonagiunta Orbiciani in Mon. 120, I, 29), *serea* (Tommaso da Faenza in Mon. 109, 52, and Rugieri d'Amici in Mon. 48, C, 20), *sarea* (Ristoro d'Arezzo in Mon. 139, 33).

Elsewhere in Italy, *cantaria* is the normal form of this particular type of conditional, used in Old Tuscan as well as in Southern and Northern dialects. The *-ia* ending conforms to normal phonological development in some regions of the South where $\bar{e}$ becomes *i* (*habēre* > Sicil. *avire*, *tēla* > Sicil. *tila*), and is, moreover, in agreement with Provençal and Ibero-Romance developments (cf. Provençal *cantaria*, Spanish *cantaría*). It is a debatable question what the exact point of origin of the *-ia* conditional is. It is tempting to see in it a Sicilian form which has penetrated into the poetic language of Tuscany "sulle ale della lirica", to quote Schiaffini. But Rohlfs (*op. cit.* § 593) raises some doubts concerning this explanation, mainly in view of the fact that the future and the conditional are not in common usage in the South. Rohlfs seems to adopt a theory of Provençal origin, but leaves the question open to doubt. A change of *-ea* to *-ia* could, of course, be attributed to the position of *e* in hiatus (cf. *vĭa* > *via*); this is the explanation that Menéndez Pidal offers for the Spanish ending, and which most scholars give for Provençal.

Conditionals in *-ia* are common in Old Tuscan: *voria, saria, averia, seria, vorriano*, etc. Old Sienese has *-ie, -ieno*: *dovrie, potrien*.

111. *Separable conditional forms.* Parallel to the separable future forms, there are instances of similar conditional formations in Northern Italian dialects. In the examples of this construction, all quoted from Rohlfs (*op. cit.* § 601), the auxiliary precedes: *have dar* (= *darebbe*), *havem fa* (= *faremmo*), *lo mondo avo perir* (= *perirebbe*).

112. *The pluperfect indicative used as a conditional.* This usage is particularly common with *fora* (< *fŭerat*) which is encountered in Dante (Purg. 26, 25) and Petrarca. It is essentially a Southern feature which has spread to other regions, such as Arezzo, Lucca and Tuscany. Guittone has *amara* (= *amerei*), *convenera* (= *converrebbe*), *credera*, etc., Bonagiunta has *portara, sembrara*, and Rinaldo d'Aquino has *finera* (= *finirebbe*). The precise geographical origin of this form may again be difficult to pin down, however, the more so as this is quite a frequent construction in Old Provençal; cf. Old Provençal *cantera, cobrera, volgra, fora*.

INDEX

(numbers refer to paragraphs)

With a few exceptions, no reference is made to forms treated in the study of endings because of the very general nature of these phenomena. The index covers only Italian verb forms. The following abbreviations are used:

Inf. = infinitive
PI = present indicative
PS = present subjunctive
Imp. = imperative
Impf. = imperfect indicative
Impf. S. = imperfect subjunctive
Pf. = perfect
PP = past participle
Pr.P. = present participle
Ger. = gerund
F = future
C = conditional
PL.I. = original pluperfect indicative used as a conditional.

Aborrire. PI 4.
accendere. Pf. 84. PP 95.
affliggere. PP 97.
aggrandire. Inf. 4.
aiutare. Inf. 19, 20. PI 19. PS 19. Impf. 19. Pr.P. 19.
albare. PP 94.
amare. PL.I. 112.
andare, ire. PI 34, 42. PS 34. Imp. 53, 54. Pf. 69. C 109.
annuire. Inf. 8.
apparire. Inf. 6. PI 4.
applaudire. Inf. 8. PI 4.
aprire. Inf. 4, 8, 84. Pf. 84. PP 97, 99.
ardere. Inf. 6, 7. Pf. 83. PP 95.

arrogere. Inf. 7.
ascondere, nascondere. Pf. 84. PP 84, 95, 100.
assumere. PP 99.
avere. Inf. 6, 8, 90. PI 38, 39, 40, 42, 43, 45, 46, 52. PS 25, 52. Imp. 56. Impf. 59. Pf. 65, 70, 78, 85, 109. PP 90. F 104, 105, 106. C 109.
avvertire. Inf. 4.

Bere. PI 77. Pf. 77. PP 90.

Cadere. Inf. 6. PI 26, 71. PS 52. Pf. 71, 77. PP 90. F 104.
cantare. Inf. 3. PI 3, 31, 32, 33,

34, 35, 36. PS 48. Imp. 53, 54. Impf. 3, 57, 58. Impf. S. 11, 60. Pf. 63, 65, 66. PP 88. F 103. C 110.
capire. Inf. 4, 6, 8. PP 97.
cedere. PP 91, 95.
cercare. Inf. 15. PI 15.
chiedere. Inf. 14, 26, 30. PI 14, 26, 30. Impf. 14. PP 100 Ger. 14.
chiudere. Inf. 18. PI 26. Pf. 83. PP 95, 100.
cogliere, corre. Inf. 10, 29, 99. PI 11, 28, 29, 99. Pf. 29, 84. PP 29, 99.
compiere, compire. Inf. 6, 7, 8, 90. PP 90.
concepire. Inf. 8.
conoscere. PI 30. Pf. 77.
consumare. Inf. 5.
convenire. PL.I. 112.
convertire. Inf. 8.
coprire. Inf. 4, 17, 18. PI 17. PP 97.
corre, see *cogliere.*
correre. Pf. 84. PP 95.
covare. PP 88.
credere. Inf. 3. PI 3, 26, 33, 34, 35, 36. Impf. 3. Impf. S. 60. Pf. 67, 85. Ger. 101. Pr.P. 102. PL.I. 112.
crepare. Inf. 13. PI 13. PP 88.
crescere. PI 30. Pf. 77.
cucire. Inf. 7, 8, 18, 81. PI 8, 30.
cuocere. Inf. 16. PI 16, 30. Impf. 16. Pf. 83, 96. PP 91, 96.

Dare. Inf. 5, 10. PI 34, 36, 39, 40, 41, 42, 43, 46. PS 52. Imp. 53, 54. Pf. 65, 68, 69, 72, 85, 86. F 105.
desinare. Inf. 19, 20. PI 19. Impf. 19.
destare. PI 11.
difendere. Pf. 84. PP 95.
digerire. Inf. 8.
digiunare. Inf. 19. PI 19, 20.
dimorare. PI 11.
dire. Inf. 10. PI 30. Imp. 54. Impf. S. 60. Pf. 70, 71, 83. PP 96, 97.
discendere. PP 95.
dispiacere. PI 11.
divertire. Inf. 4.
dividere. PP 95.
dolere. Inf. 8, 16. PI 16, 28. PS 28. Impf. 16. Pf. 80, 84, 96. PP 96, 99. F 104.
domare. PP 88.
dormire. Inf. 4, 18, 102. PI 23. Pr.P. 102.
dovere. Inf. 21. PI 21, 25, 26, 39, 47. PS 52. Impf. S. 60. Pf. 67. PP 90. F 104. C 109.
durre (Old Italian). Pf. 83. PP 97.

Empiere, empire. Inf. 6.
erigere. PP 99.
essere. Inf. 7. PI 31, 34, 36, 38, 92. PS 34, 48, 52. Imp. 56. Impf. 38, 59. Impf. S. 61. Pf. 61, 72, 82. PP 92. F 105, 106. C 110. PL.I. 112.
evadere. PP 95.
evitare. PI 11.

Fallire. Inf. 8. PP 93.
fare. Inf. 5, 10. PI 24, 38, 40, 41, 42, 43, 46. PS 24, 52. Imp. 53, 54. Impf. S. 60. Pf. 36, 52, 61, 63, 70, 71, 72, 78, 85. PP 97. F 105. C 110.
fendere. PP 91.
ferire, fiedere. Inf. 7, 26, 30. PI 12, 26, 30. Impf. 12.
fiedere, see *ferire.*
figgere. PP 95.
fingere. Inf. 27. Pf. 83, 84. PP 97, 98.
finire. Inf. 4. PI 4. PP 89, 93. PL.I. 112.
fiorire. Inf. 4, 6, 8.
fir (Old Italian). Inf. 106. F 106.
fondere. PP 95.
fornire. Inf. 9.
frangere. Inf. 98. PI 26, 27, 98. Pf. 84. PP 98.
friggere. Pf. 83.
fuggire. Inf. 4, 7, 8. PI 24, 26, 39.

Gemere. PI 13. F 13.
gettare, gittare. Inf. 15. PI 15. Pf. 15.
giacere. Inf. 90. Pf. 76. PP 90.
giovare. PP 88.

INDEX

gire, see *andare, ire.*
gittare, see *gettare.*
giungere. PI 26, 27. Pf. 83, 84. PP 97.
godere. Pf. 67.
guadagnare. Inf. 9.
guardare. Inf. 9.
guarire. Inf. 9.
guarnire. Inf. 9.
guastare. PP 94.

Immergere. PP 95.
intridere. Pf. 84.
invadere. PP 95.
ire, see *andare.*
irritare. PI 11.

Leggere. Pf. 84. PP 91, 97.
levare. Inf. 14. PI 14.
lodare. Inf. 18. PP 88. Ger. 101. Pr.P. 102.

Mancare. PI 30.
mangiare. Inf. 20. PI 20. Impf. 20.
mantenere. Inf. 27.
menovare (Old Italian). Inf. 5.
mentire. PI 4.
mescere. Inf. 6.
mettere. Imp. 53. Pf. 83, 85. PP 83, 95, 96.
mietere. Inf. 14. PI 14. Impf. 14.
mordere. Inf. 6, 7. Pf. 84 PP 95.
morire. Inf. 8, 16, 18. PI 16, 24. Impf. 16. PP 97. F 104.
mungere. Inf. 6, 7. PI 30.
muovere. Inf. 6, 7, 16, 84, 95. PI 16. Impf. 16. Pf. 84, 95. PP 95, 100.

Nascere. Inf. 76. PI 30, 76. Pf. 76. PP 91, 97.
nascondere, see *ascondere.*
negare. Inf. 14. PI 14. Impf. 14.
notare. Inf. 17.
nuocere. Inf. 6, 8, 16, 90. PI 16, 24, 30. Impf. 16. Pf. 76. PP 90.
nuotare. Inf. 17. Pl 17. Impf. 17.
nutrire. Inf. 102. PI 4. Pr.P. 102.

Offendere. Pf. 84. PP 95.
offrire. Inf. 4, 6, 8, 84. Pf. 84. PP 99.

opprimere. PP 95.
osare. Inf. 18. PP 94.

Pagare. PI 30.
parere. PI 24. Pf. 80, 84. PP 91, 95. Pr.P. 80, 102. F 104.
partire. Inf. 3, 4. PI 3, 4, 65. PS 48. Impf. 3, 57, 65. Impf. S. 60. Pf. 65. PP 89. Ger. 101. Pr.P. 102. F 103.
patire. PI 4.
pentire. Inf. 4, 6, 8. PP 93.
perdere. Impf. S. 60. Pf. 69, 84, 90. PP 84, 90, 91, 95.
perire. PI 4.
persuadere. Pf. 83.
pesare. Inf. 15. PI 15.
piacere. Inf. 8. PI 24. Pf. 76.
piangere. Inf. 27. PI 27. Pf. 83, 84, 99. PP 97, 99.
pingere. Pf. 83, 84. PP 98.
piovere. Inf. 90. PI 77, 90. Pf. 77. PP 90.
porgere. PP 99.
porre. Inf. 10. PI 27, 81. Impf. 27. **Pf. 81. PP 90, 95, 100.**
portare. PP. 88. PL. I. 112.
potere. PI 44, 52, 67, 90. PS 52. Pf. 67, 79, 85. PP 90. F 103, 104. C 109.
preferire. Inf. 4.
pregare. Inf. 13. PI 13.
premere. Pf. 95. PP 95.
prendere. Pf. 84. PP 84, 95.
profferire. Inf. 8.
prostrare. Inf. 5.
provare. Inf. 17. PI 17.
prudere. Inf. 7.
pungere. Pf. 84.
putire. Inf. 8.

Radere. Pf. 83.
rapire. Inf. 7, 8.
redimere. PP 99.
reggere. Pf. 96. PP 96, 97.
rendere. Pf. 69, 84. PP 84, 91, 95.
ricevere. PI 11. PP 99.
ridere. Inf. 6, 7. Pf. 83. PP 95.
riedere. Inf. 7. PI 12. Impf. 12.
rilucere. Inf. 6, 7.
rimanere. PI 27, 52. PS 52. Pf. 83. PP 95, 100.

rinverdire. Inf. 4.
rispondere. Inf. 6, 7. Pf. 81, 84. PP 100.
ritenere. PI 11.
rodere. Pf. 83.
rompere. Impf. S. 60. Pf. 77, 85.
rubare. Inf. 18. PI 18.

Salire. Inf. 4, 28, 102. PI 28, 34. Imp. 53. Impf. S. 60. Pf. 65, 84. Pr. P. 102.
sapere. Inf. 6, 102. PI 24, 39, 46, 102. PS 24, 52. Imp. 56. Pf. 78, 85. PP 90. Pr. P. 102. F 104.
scegliere, scerre. Inf. 10. PI 11. Pf. 84. PP 99.
scerpare. Inf. 5.
scerre, see *scegliere.*
sciogliere, sciorre. Inf. 10, 29. PI 29. Pf. 29. PP 29.
scrivere. Inf. 84, 95. PI 31, 32. PS 48, 50. Imp. 53, 54. Impf. S. 11, 60. Pf. 65, 71, 83, 84, 95. PP. 97.
scuotere. Inf. 16. PI 16. Impf. 16.
sedere. Inf. 12. PI 12, 16. Impf. 12. PP 12, 90.
segare. Inf. 14. PI 14. Impf. 14. PP 88.
seguire. Inf. 4, 8, 14. PI 14. Impf. 14.
sembrare. PL. I. 112.
sentire. Inf. 4, 6, 102. PI 33, 34, 35, 36. PS 48, 51. Imp. 54. Pf. 69. PP 93. Pr. P. 102.
seppellire PP 97.
servire. Inf. 4. PI 4, 23, 31, 32. PP 93.
smarrire. Inf. 9.
soffrire. Inf. 4, 8, 18. PP 99.
solere. Inf. 16. PI 16, 28. Impf. 16. F 104.
solvere. PP 99.
sonare Inf. 16. PI 16. Impf. 16. PP 88.
sorgere. Pf. 99. PP 99.
spargere. PP 95.
sparire. Inf. 6. Pf. 80.
spegnere, spengere. PI 27.
splendere. Inf. 6.
stare. Inf. 5, 10. PI 34, 39, 40, 42, 43, 46. PS 52. Imp. 53, 54.

Pf. 68, 72 ,77, 85, 86. PP 92. F 105.
sternutare, sternutire. Inf. 5.
stringere. Pf. 83.
svellere. PI 29.

Tacere. Inf. 8. PI 24, 71. Pf. 71, 76.
temere. PI 23, 52. PS 49, 52. Imp. 53. Impf. S. 60. Pf. 67, 71. Ger. 101. Pr. P. 102.
tendere. Pf. 84. PP 84.
tenere. Inf. 12, 27. PI 12, 26, 27, 52. PS 52. Impf. 12, 27. Impf. S. 60. Pf. 77, 84. PP 90, 93. F 104.
tergere. Inf. 6. PP 95.
toccare. PP 94.
togliere, torre. Inf. 10, 29. PI 29. Pf. 29, 84. PP 29, 99.
tonare. PP 88.
tondere. Inf. 6.
torcere. Inf. 6.
torre, see *togliere.*
tossire. PI 4.
tradire. Inf. 7. PI 4.
traggere, trarre. Inf. 5, 10. PS 52. Pf. 83. PP 94, 97.
trasparire. Inf. 6.
tremare. Inf. 5, 13. PI 13.
trovare. Inf. 17. PI 17. PP 94.

Ubbidire. Inf. 4, 102. Pr. P. 102.
uccidere. Pf. 84.
udire. Inf. 6, 18. PI 18. PS 48. PP 18, 89. F 104.
usare. PP 94.
uscire. Inf. 4, 21. PI 21, 30.

Valere. PI 28, 90. PS 28, 52, 90. Pf. 84, 90. PP 90, 91, 95. Pr. P. 102. F 104.
vedere. Inf. 3. PI 3, 23, 26, 32, 33, 34, 35, 36, 52, 90, 101, 102. PS 52. Imp. 53, 54. Impf. 3, 57. Impf. S. 60. Pf. 79, 85, 90. PP 90, 91, 100. Ger. 101. Pr. P. 102. F 103, 104.
vendere, PI 11. Pf. 68, 69. PP 90.
venire. Inf. 12, 102. PI 12, 26, 27, 40, 52. PS 52. Impf. 12. Impf.

S. 60. Pf. 77, 84. PP 27, 91, 93.
Pr. P. 102. F 104.
vestire. Inf. 4. PP 93.
vietare. Inf. 14. PI 14. PP 88.
vincere. Pf. 84. PP 98.
vivere. Pf. 90, 96. PP 90, 96, 99.
volare. Inf. 17. PI 17.

volere. Inf. 16. PI 16, 28, 31, 44, 45, 101. Imp. 56. Impf. 16. Pf. 77, 80, 84. PP 90, 91. Ger. 101. Pr. P. 102. F 103, 104.
volgere. PI 29. PP 99.
votare. Inf. 17.
vuotare. Inf. 17. PI 17. Impf. 17.

BIBLIOGRAPHY

BATTISTI, C., and ALESSIO, G. *Dizionario etimologico italiano*. Firenze: Barbèra, 1950-1957.
BERTONI, GIULIO. *Profilo linguistico d'Italia*. Modena: Società Tipografica Modenese, 1940.
———. "Postille al Libro dei Banchieri", *Giornale storico della litteratura italiana*, LIV (1909), 269-273.
BONFANTE, G. "The Latin and Romance weak perfect", *Language*, XVII (1942), 201-211.
BOURCIEZ, ED. *Éléments de linguistique romane*. Paris: Klincksieck, 1956.
CAIX, N. "Sull'influenza dell'accento nella coniugazione *manducare, adiutare*", *Giornale di filologia romanza*, II (1879), 10-18.
CRESCINI, VINCENZO. *Manuale per l'avviamento agli studi provenzali*. Milano: Hoepli, 1926.
DANTE ALIGHIERI. *La Divina Commedia*. Milano: Biblioteca Universale Rizzoli, 1949.
DIONISOTTI, C., and GRAYSON, C. *Early Italian Texts*. Oxford: Basil Blackwell, 1949.
D'OVIDIO, F., and MEYER-LÜBKE, W. *Grammatica storica della lingua e dei dialetti italiani*. Milano: Hoepli, 1932.
———. "Ancora sulla etimologia delle forme grammaticali italiane *amano, dicono* ecc.", *Zeitschrift für Romanische Philologie*, XXIII (1899), 313-320.
ELCOCK, W. D. *The Romance Languages*. London: Faber and Faber, 1960.
FÖRSTER, W. "Die toskanische Endung -'a/ono der 3. Pluralis Praesentis", *Zeitschrift für Romanische Philologie*, XXII (1898), 521-525.
FORNACIARI, RAFFAELLO. *Grammatica della lingua italiana*. Firenze: Sansoni, 1936.
FOUCHÉ, PIERRE. *Morphologie Historique du Français. Le Verbe*. Paris: Klincksieck, 1967.
GARTNER, TH.: "*Die, diemo, dino*". *Zeitschrift für Romanische Philologie*, XXXI (1907), 234-236.
GRANDGENT, C. H. *An Introduction to Vulgar Latin*. Boston: D. C. Heath, 1907.
———. *From Latin to Italian*. Cambridge: Harvard University Press, 1927.
HALL, ROBERT A. *Bibliografia della linguistica italiana*. Firenze: Sansoni, 1958.
KUHN, ALWIN. *Romanische Philologie*. Bern: Francke Verlag, 1951.
LAUSBERG, HEINRICH. *Romanische Sprachwissenschaft*. 4 vols. Berlin: W. de Gruyter, 1958-1962.

MARCHESINI, E. "I perfetti italiani in -*etti*", *Studî di filologia romanza*, I (1855), 445-448.
―――. "Note filologiche", *Studî di filologia romanza*, II (1887), 1-30.
MAURER, T. H., JR. "The Romance Conjugation in -*ēscō* (-*īscō*) -*īre*", *Language*, XXVII (1951), 136-145.
MENÉNDEZ PIDAL, R. *Manual de Gramática Histórica Española*. Madrid: Espasa-Calpe, 1952.
MERLO, C. "Gli italiani *amano, dicono* e gli odierni dialetti umbro-romaneschi", *Studî romanzi*, VI (1909), 69-83.
MEYER-LÜBKE, W. *Einführung in das Studium der romanischen Sprachwissenschaft*. Heidelberg: Winter, 1920.
―――. *Grammaire des Langues Romanes*. Paris-Leipzig: Welter, 1890-1895.
―――. *Grammatica storica della lingua italiana e dei dialetti toscani*. Torino: Loescher 1964.
MIGLIORINI, BRUNO. *Storia della Lingua Italiana*. Firenze: Sansoni, 1961.
MONACI, ERNESTO. *Crestomazia italiana dei primi secoli*. Roma - Napoli - Città di Castello: Società editrice Dante Alighieri, 1955.
NYROP, KR. *Grammaire Historique de la Langue Française*. 6 vols. Copenhagen: Gyldendal, 1924-1930.
PEI, MARIO A. *The Italian Language*. New York: Columbia University Press, 1941.
ROHLFS, GERHARD. *Historische Grammatik der Italienischen Sprache*. 3 vols. Bern: Francke Verlag, 1949-1954.
―――. *Romanische Philologie*. Heidelberg: C. Winter, 1952.
―――. *Vom Vulgärlatein zum Altfranzösischen*. Tübingen: Max Niemeyer Verlag, 1960.
RUBENBAUER, H., and HOFMAN, J. B. *Lateinische Grammatik auf sprachwissenschaftlicher Grundlage*. München ― Berlin: R. Oldenburg, 1944.
SCHIAFFINI, A. *Testi fiorentini del Dugento e dei primi del Trecento*. Firenze: Sansoni, 1954.
SCHMID, H. *Zur Formenbildung von* dare *und* stare *im Romanischen*. Bern, 1949.
SCHÜRMANN, J. *Die Entstehung und Verbreitung der sogenannten "Verkürzten Participien" im Romanischen*. Strassburg, 1890.
STOLZ, F., and DEBRUNNER, A., and SCHMID, W. P. *Geschichte der lateinischen Sprache*. Berlin: W. de Gruyter, 1966.
TRABALZA, C. *Storia della grammatica italiana*. Bologna: Forni, 1963.
VÄÄNANEN, VEIKKO. *Introduction au Latin Vulgaire*. Paris: Klincksieck, 1963.
VOSSLER, KARL. *Einführung ins Vulgärlatein*. München, 1955.
WAGNER, M. L. *Historische Lautlehre des Sardischen*. Beiheft 93, *Zeitschrift für Romanische Philologie*, Halle, 1941.
WAHLGREN, E. G. "Étude sur les actions analogiques réciproques du parfait et du participe passé dans les langues romanes", *Uppsala Universitetets Årsskrift*, Uppsala, 1920.
WIESE, BERTHOLD. *Altitalienisches Elementarbuch*. Heidelberg: Winter, 1904.
WILLIAMS, EDWIN B. *From Latin to Portuguese*. Philadelphia: University of Pennsylvania Press, 1962.
ZAUNER, A. *Romanische Sprachwissenschaft*. Berlin: W. de Gruyter, 1921-1926.
ZIMMERMANN, A. "Zum -*utus* Partizip im Romanischen", *Zeitschrift für Romanische Philologie*, XXVIII (1904), 97.

The Department of Romance Studies Digital Arts and Collaboration Lab at the University of North Carolina at Chapel Hill is proud to support the digitization of the North Carolina Studies in the Romance Languages and Literatures series.

www.ingramcontent.com/pod-product-compliance
Lightning Source LLC
Chambersburg PA
CBHW020421230426
43663CB00007BA/1266